TWAYNE'S WORLD AUTHORS SERIES

A Survey of the World's Literature

Sylvia E. Bowman, Indiana University

GENERAL EDITOR

FRANCE

Maxwell A. Smith, Guerry Professor of French, Emeritus
The University of Chattanooga
Former Visiting Professor in Modern Languages
The Florida State University

EDITOR

Pierre Loti

(TWAS 285)

PIERRE LOTI

Pierre Loti

By MICHAEL G. LERNER

University of Glasgow

Twayne Publishers, Inc.   ::   New York

843.89
V 623 z L

ISBN 0–8057–2546–6

170681

Preface

During his lifetime the exotic travels, idyllic romances, and strange personality of Pierre Loti earned him an almost mythical reputation not only in France, but in Europe as a whole; he excited the imagination of a vast reading public and captured the hearts of an audience that was largely feminine and often royal. Today, fifty years after his death, this cult has virtually faded away along with the outlook and emotions of the age that created it; the imaginative thrill and gentle nostalgia fostered by Loti's novels are now often considered excessive and shallow by a modern reader for whom the mystery of overseas has been largely destroyed and from whose world the magic of Romanticism has almost been banished. But even if the cult of Loti has suffered from changes in the twentieth century, the myth of Loti as he created it in his novels and diaries still lives on; such were the secrecy and artifice of Loti and such has been the largely uncritical allegiance of most of his commentators that no comprehensive critical study exists on him. Without intending to destroy the myth, it is aimed in the present study, the first in English, to provide an analysis of Loti's work against the fascinating background of his life, using all the data available, and to set Loti in the moral context of his period, emphasizing his contemporaneity as well as his individuality. In this way it is hoped that there will be revealed beyond his mythical reputation a mind, imagination, and style worthy of the closer consideration of modern scholars and more interesting to the reading world of today.

Acknowledgments are due to the publishers of Loti's works and correspondence for permitting my use of these; the translation of extracts quoted here is my own. I should also like to record my thanks to the staff of the British Museum and Bibliothèque Nationale for their assistance in my research; to the University of Glasgow for a grant to visit Rochefort; and to M. André Moulis and Mme E. Loti-Viaud for their generous help to my documentation.

Finally, I dedicate this study as a tribute to both the living and the dead: to my parents whose understanding was often demanded, but whose patience never failed; and to the men, women, and children who were martyrs of the Nazi tyranny and whose inhuman and unjust fate should never be erased from the minds of men; may each of these examples from both the recent past and the present serve as inspirations for the future.

MICHAEL G. LERNER

London, England

Contents

Chronology

1850 January 14: Pierre Loti born Louis Marie Julien Viaud at Rochefort (Saintonge).
1861– Attends Collège de Rochefort.
1866
1865 March 10: Gustave Viaud dies in Indo-China, age 27.
1866– Théodore Viaud is accused of embezzlement and left in debt.
1868
1866– Julien joins the Navy and attends the Lycée Henri IV in Paris.
1867
1867 October 1: Julien a cadet on the "Borda" at Brest.
1869 October 8: Embarks as a midshipman, 2nd class, on the "Jean Bart" and cruises in the Mediterranean and off the Americas.
1870 June 8: Théodore Viaud dies, age 66. Julien seeks to support his mother and aunts and buy the family house for them. August 8: Julien, now a midshipman, 1st class, patrolling in the Baltic and North Sea during the Franco-German War.
1871 May 18: Leaves on the "Vaudreuil" for South America and the Pacific.
1872 January–March: At Tahiti on the "Flore."
1873– In Senegal. Breaks with his friend Joseph Bernard.
1874
1875 January–July: Takes course at Joinville gymnasium.
1876– Leaves on the "Couronne" for Salonica and is stationed on the
1877 "Gladiateur" at Istanbul.
1877– On the "Tonnerre" and "Moselle" cruising off Britanny and Normandy. Begins friendship with Pierre Le Cor.
1879
1879 January: *Aziyadé* published by Calmann-Lévy in Paris.
1880– In the Mediterranean and at Cherbourg, Rochefort, or Toulon on the
1883 "Friedland" and "Surveillante."
1880 January–February: *Le Mariage de Loti* appears in Juliette Adam's *Nouvelle Revue*.
1881 February 24: Loti becomes *lieutenant de vaisseau*. March–May: *Le Roman d'un Spahi* appears in the *Nouvelle Revue*.
1883 May 29: Loti embarks on the "Atalante" for Annam. August–September: *Mon Frère Yves* appears in the *Revue des Deux Mondes*. December 14: Loti is recalled to France on the "Corrèze" after his articles on the Annam War appear in *Le Figaro*.

1884 March 20: Leaves again for the Far East on the "Mytho"; cf. *Propos d'Exil.*

1885 July–November: Visits Japan on the "Triomphante"; cf. *Madame Chrysanthème, Japoneries d'Automne.*

1886 March–June: *Pêcheur d'Islande* appears in the *Nouvelle Revue.* October 20: Loti marries Jeanne Blanche Franc de Ferrière.

1886– Works at the naval depot at Rochefort and decorates the rooms in
1888 the old house in exotic styles.

1887 July 15: Receives *Légion d'Honneur.* September 27: Visits the Queen of Rumania, Carmen Silva, at Sinaia; cf. *L'Exilée.* Stops at Istanbul on return; cf. *Fantôme d'Orient.*

1888– Loti in command of the "Ecureuil" at Rochefort. Close friendship
1890 with Léo Thémèze.

1889 March 18: Samuel Loti-Viaud is born. March–May: Loti in Morocco; cf. *Au Maroc.*

1891– In command of the gunboat "Javelot" in the Bidassoa area. Lives at
1898 Hendaye and enjoys Basque life; cf. *Ramuntcho.*

1892 April 7: Received at the Académie Française.

1894 February–May: Makes a pilgrimage through Arabia to Jerusalem and the Middle East; cf. *Le Désert, Jérusalem, La Galilée.*

1896 November 12: Nadine Viaud dies, age 86.

1899 November: Loti begins a tour of Ceylon and India; cf. *L'Inde sans les Anglais.*

1900 April–June: Loti leaves India and crosses the Persian desert toward Isfahan and Teheran; cf. *Vers Ispahan.* August 2: Leaves on the "Redoutable" for China and Japan; cf. *Les Derniers Jours de Pékin, La Troisième Jeunesse de Madame Prune.*

1901 November 23: Loti lands at Saigon and sets off for Angkor Wat; cf. *Pèlerin d'Angkor.*

1903– In command of the cruiser "Vautour" at Istanbul; cf. *Les Désen-*
1904 *chantées.*

1905– Loti, now *capitaine de vaisseau,* in charge of naval depot at
1906 Rochefort.

1907 January–May: Visits Egypt; cf. *La Mort de Philae.*

1909 July 5–11: Loti in London; he meets Queen Alexandra and King Edward VII.

1910 January 14: Is placed on naval retirement list. August–October: Stays in Turkey.

1912 September–October: Loti goes to New York to see a production of his play *The Daughter of Heaven.*

1913 August–September: Visits Turkey again after Balkan War and is given a hero's welcome; cf. *Turquie Agonisante, Suprêmes Visions d'Orient.*

Chronology

1914   August 3: Signs on at Rochefort for war service.

1915– Loti is attached to the staffs of Generals Galliéni and Franchet
1917   d'Esperey; visits Belgium, the Western Front, Alsace, Spain, and
       Italy; cf. *La Grande Barbarie, La Hyène Enragée.*

1918   March 15: Returns home ill and is demobilized; visits the front
       again and continues to write on the war; cf. *L'Horreur Allemande.*

1919– Campaigns in the press and in his work in favor of Turkey; cf.
1920   *La Mort de Notre Chère France en Orient.*

1923   June 10: Pierre Loti dies, age 73, on a visit to Hendaye. June 16:
       Loti is buried on the isle of St. Pierre d'Oleron near Rochefort, the
       home of his ancestors.

CHAPTER 1

Julien Viaud Midshipman

I The Viaud Family

IT was in the family home in the Rue Saint Pierre at the port of Rochefort on the banks of the Charente in the province of Saintonge, some three hundred miles southwest of Paris, that Louis Marie Julien Viaud, later known as Pierre Loti, was born on 14 January 1850. His mother Nadine was the younger daughter of Henriette Renaudin and Philippe Texier,[1] a naval administrator on the Isle of Oleron at the mouth of the Charente near La Rochelle, where the Huguenot Renaudin family had resettled after the persecutions which had exiled them to Britain and Holland more than a century before. After her father's premature death, she had lived with her sister and mother on Oleron[2] near the Renaudin ancestral home until, on a visit to Rochefort, she met her future husband Jean Théodore Viaud, an official in the *mairie* of local provincial stock. Timid and sensitive, she was attracted by his interest in music and poetry and reputation as a self-made man of letters and playwright, and married him in August, 1830.

They then settled in the Texier family home in the town, "the most ordinary of small towns" as Loti was to call it later in *Le Roman d'un Enfant,* with its small white houses and quiet streets surrounded by flat, open countryside offering occasional glimpses of the sea. Although Jean Théodore Viaud was originally Catholic, he had, like Philippe Texier before him, been converted to the sober, puritan Protestantism of the Huguenot strain in Nadine's family. Their life was then simple and pious though not deprived of the modest comforts afforded by Jean Théodore's rise in the municipal administration. When Julien was born, his parents were over forty and already had a daughter, Marie, of nineteen and a son, Gustave, of twelve; and the household included Nadine's mother Henriette, her sister Clarisse, and her aunt Rosalie (the Tante Claire and Tante Berthe of *Le Roman d'un Enfant*) as well as, in Loti's infancy, Théodore's senile mother Marie-Anne

Morillon. It is not surprising then that the new arrival was thoroughly spoilt and was soon to become a delicate, cosseted "indoor plant," a "rare little hothouse bloom"; Loti wrote later in *Prime Jeunesse:*

> One of the great misfortunes of my life was without doubt to have been so much younger than all those in my family who loved me and whom I loved too; to have arrived among them like a sort of small Benjamin on whom all their bountiful affections were destined to converge.

This circumstance was further encouraged by the "excessive intellectual and sentimental nurturing with which the strange blooms that were Nadine's children were raised."[3] Beneath the quiet surface of the family's rather austere existence, there seethed those sublimated forces of anxious emotion and imagination that were to mold and motivate Loti's personality forever. The Renaudin and Texier families had always been extremely close-knit because of their past of persecution and exile, and their members had always displayed an intense spirit of togetherness; Nadine was no exception to this and she passed on to her children her extremely nervous, anxious, emotional sensibility fused with her scrupulous Protestant sense of responsibility; it is she who worries over and largely writes to Marie when the latter spends some months in Paris in 1851, 1852, and 1854 to study art and stays in Switzerland and Germany and again when Gustave leaves for Bordeaux in 1858 to train as a naval surgeon; and it will be with her and Marie that Loti will correspond for much of his life. In the adult world of Loti's infancy, she is the supreme protective figure, in whose skirts he can hide and in whose arms he can find the most complete refuge from his isolation; he describes her in *Le Roman d'un Enfant* as: "... a figure that was quite unique, whom I was never inclined to compare to any other and from whom for me, there radiated all happiness, security and tenderness and there derived all that was good including my nascent faith and prayer..." While she epitomized the intense family protectiveness and Huguenot piety Loti later described in *Le Roman d'un Enfant* and *Prime Jeunesse* and longed to regain in later life, Théodore Viaud represented by both his own writing of poetry, plays, and a history of Rochefort and his encouragement of Marie's artistic talents a highly imaginative but more sober, creative literary spirit, which matched a keen attention to facts with an equally keen sense of humor. Both Protestant visionary emotion and scrupulousness were thus fused in the nervous temperament and artistic sensibility Loti was to inherit from his family background and that was already evident in Marie's writing and painting, which so impressed her young brother as he shows in *Prime Jeunesse* (Chapter V).

II *Loti's Childhood*

Loti's childhood was by no means as melancholy as it appears from the works he afterward devoted to it with great nostalgia. For even if the family's life was simple and pious and included evening prayers from the 1764 Bible and visits to the temple, it also offered young Loti plenty of opportunity to play with his aunt, Marie, or his sisterly friend Lucie Duplais on the estate of La Limoise, three miles from Rochefort. He later wrote in *Fleurs d'Ennui:*

> Just the very name *La Limoise* is able to evoke for me as in a trance the scenes and impressions of my childhood world of long ago: forests of oak trees, open heathland, a stony countryside with an age-old pastoral look about it, flocks of sheep and the scent of thyme in the air. I could write volumes on this small area of land and I would not be able to convey accurately in words the charm it held for me as a child full of imagination.

This contact with Nature and the simplicity of his home life encouraged him, as it did his elders, to indulge his imagination, to seek "refuge in a realm of fancy, a fairyland of which he was the fairy prince,"[4] and become a hero of romance. The family's reading of the Bible, in fact, initiated young Loti's flights of fancy with its grandiose descriptions of the Creation and Apocalypse as he recalled in *Le Roman d'un Enfant.* Furthermore, it was Loti's imaginative cult of his Huguenot ancestors and their traditions, seen later in his play *Judith Renaudin,* that maintained his faith and attached him to his family particularly on the isle of Oleron, as is seen on his visit there in 1867, described in *Prime Jeunesse* (Chapter L), to see the remaining members of his family there, his aunts Clara and Célina Lieutier and their aged mother, his great aunt Clarisse; it even made him think, under Marie's encouragement, of becoming a pastor.

Moreover, young Loti's reading of a monthly paper on missionary work overseas soon linked this religious romance with his cult of the exotic. This had grown out of his exciting reading on the ancient world, particularly Egypt, and his looking at the pictures of scenes of tropical splendor in various books given him; it also derived from his fascination with exotic things—his great-uncle Henri Tageau's shell collection and his own "museum" of butterflies and shells. And just as the little boy's romantic imagination had compensated for the cold, uninspiring monotony of worship at the temple by converting it into a cult of his ancestors and family heritage, so he soon transformed his walks in the garden of La Limoise or the forest of Saint Porchaire, where his sister lived since her marriage on 25 August 1864 to Armand Bon, into the adventures of a Redskin or a trapper, following his reading of Chateaubriand, and longed for the exciting colors and luxuriance of the colonies in contrast to the remote dullness of Rochefort.

This cult gained momentum by the arrival of Loti's brother, a ship's surgeon on the "Infatigable," at Tahiti in June, 1859, and the letters and photographs, the first ever taken of the island,[5] he received from Gustave out there.

It is not surprising that in this family, this "circle of anxious, tender hearts," where the absence of one of its sons maintained an obsessively sentimental gloom, where each letter that arrived was received with desperate joy, and where any lack of correspondence caused virtual hysteria, a young child's cult of his elder brother's life overseas should have so dominated his imagination that it distracted him at the school, the *pension* Bernard Palissy, which he attended for two years until 1861. He wrote to Gustave at that time:

I would love to be with you there in Tahiti; it seems to me it must be so nice over there; better than here at school. . . . Imagine the difference between spending one's days amid lovely flowers and being stuck here on a bench! If one thinks of Tahiti for a moment, one gets punished with lines. I've got quite a few for that.[6]

And just as Gustave's empty room evoked her son for Nadine Viaud by its associations on which her visionary imagination liked to embroider, and everything of her brother was sacred for Marie in her dreams of overseas, so the little pond Gustave had built for his brother while on leave from September to December, 1862, before his departure for Indo-China and the exotic gifts he sent him became the object of a fetishistic sentimentalism for Loti and symbols of his desire for adventure. Young Loti, too, wanted to participate in those exotic scenes that could at the moment only be created in the scenery of the miniature theater he managed with his friend Jeanne; he disliked being a day boy at the Collège de Rochefort after 1861 just as much as the private tutors he had had at home; timid and reserved, he escaped the classroom in his imagination and by the age of fourteen wrote to his brother asking about the possibility of his joining the Navy. He had read of one of his ancestor's life at sea in a logbook of 1813 he had found at home and had seen and heard the sailors in the streets of Rochefort; he now wanted to escape and see the world like his big brother.

III   *In the Navy*

Loti's plan to follow in his brother's footsteps were halted by Gustave's death on 10 March 1865 from anemia, contracted during his stay at Paolo Condor in Indo-China, and his burial at sea in the Bay of Bengal; clearly, his mother did not want now to risk losing her other son to the deep. Circumstances at home were, however, to cause a change in his parents' attitude and allow this very small, quiet, and fragile youth of fifteen to pursue the course his imagination rather than his physique had directed him toward. In 1866 Théodore Viaud as *receveur municipal,* is accused of mislaying fourteen thousand francs in bonds in the town's finances; he loses his job on 2 June 1866, and for a few days he is imprisoned. He is in fact not exculpated until a court hearing in February, 1868; by then, however, he had accumulated a series of heavy debts. The result of this calamity in the strict, sober Viaud household was an ever greater need to economize; the family home at Rochefort had to take in lodgers, and its domestic staff and equipment had to be severely reduced. Loti, as he shows in Chapter **XXXI** of *Prime Jeunesse,* was terribly shocked and upset by this destruction of his home; spoilt and full of romantic fancies in his childhood, Loti had, moreover, partly through an innate timidity, been rather aloof at school and this sudden poverty and sight of his father in prison struck a heavy blow at his self-respect, which he did his utmost to reestablish later in life. For the moment, he had

to resign himself to it. Similarly, his parents had to resign themselves to the fact that they could not afford to allow their remaining
son to continue his studies at the Ecole Polytechnique; they therefore consented to his joining the Navy in October, 1866.

In doing so, Loti was, like his brother, continuing a family naval
tradition; his paternal grandfather had been on the "Achilles" and
died of wounds received at Trafalgar (1805)—although it has since
been claimed he died of typhoid in Spain—his father's brother had
perished after the shipwreck of the "Méduse" (1816), and his
mother's grandfather had commanded the "Vengeur" (1794). The
difference between these and Loti was that the latter was much more
sensitive and delicate—Léon Daudet was later to describe his
sensitivity as like that of the finest glass;[7] furthermore, he had been
horribly disillusioned and hurt by recent events. For Loti, joining
the Navy satisfied not only his childish desire to see faraway places,
but also his need for an opportunity to regain his own and his
family's self-respect; his self-consciousness regarding their new
situation is reflected in the very title of his memoirs of this period,
Un Jeune Officier Pauvre, as well as in the tale *Le Mur d'en Face
(Figures et Choses qui Passaient)*; he wrote later in *Matelot:*

> He suffered cruelly from seeing his mother so degraded in the quality of
> her dress, in the comfort of her home and the style of her way of life. He
> was filled with the determination and the hope that one day he would be
> able to raise her to her former station; he would resign himself to the
> ordeal just for the moment . . .

This outlook is evident in Loti's impressions of Paris during his year
there at the Lycée Henri IV. He is homesick, lonely, and poor; as he
recalls in *Fleurs d'Ennui,* he dislikes the rowdiness of his neighbors
and the bohemian life in the Latin quarter; apart from visits to the
literary salon of his aunt Nelly Lieutier-Besson, to the Opéra and
the Louvre, Loti lives isolated and escapes his solitude and ennui by
beginning his *journal intime,* which was eventually to comprise
some two hundred *cahiers.*

In July, 1867, Loti takes his entrance exams and passes, and in
the following October embarks as a cadet on board the "Borda" at
Brest. Being part of a team, climbing up ropes, and sleeping in a
hammock were new experiences for Loti, but ones which, according
to his account of them toward the end of *Prime Jeunesse*, were at

first not without fascination for him. The life on board was, however, despite the math, astronomy, dancing, and other lessons the commander provided for the cadets, fairly rough; Loti described it in *Un Jeune Officer Pauvre:*

In the floating cloister in which we youngsters had suddenly been con- fined, life was rough and austere. In many ways it resembled that of the sailors and had been introduced here for our training; like them, we spent a lot of time exposed to the wind, the spray, and the sea air which left a taste of salt on your lips; like them, we climbed up onto the yards to make the sails taut and got our hands cut in doing so. . . .

Young Loti thus injured his knee shortly after joining on and had to be constantly hospitalized because of sore throats and mumps during his first year aboard. Moreover, apart from a short cruise on the "Bougainville" up the French coast, the cadets' life was stationary and dreary; once more, Loti's dreams of overseas are not immediately realized and he writes on 23 December 1868 to his mother:

Imagine how miserable it is to be confined like this in a vessel that does not move and to have all the inconveniences of a long voyage without having any of the attractions or the variety. . . . Furthermore, we have more work than we can cope with, exhausting exercises, bad and inadequate food and never any heat. . . . And to see, on top of that, nothing but rain, continual mist, and a sea and a coastline so full of mist and looking so gloomy as to give one the spleen . . . [8]

Despite further stays in hospital and some months of convalescence at home in spring, 1869, Loti managed, however, to pass 2nd class midshipman in the following August, and by October he had embarked on the "Jean Bart" and was at last sailing toward the sun.

Loti had looked forward to leaving the training ship and exploring the world for quite some time; in November, 1868, he had written to his sister how much he longed for the end of the course:

At the end of eight months we will be undertaking a magnificent voyage to those faraway countries that have captured my imagination since my infancy . . . above all, my days as a schoolboy will be over and

I will be embarking on life itself. . . . I will be free to work at the things which please me and to pursue all my ambitions and try to realize them.[9]

Now that he was at sea, however, an outbreak of smallpox that forced the ship to return to Brest from the Canaries only a month after leaving and the burial at sea of some sailors disillusioned him a little at first. But this disquiet soon passed; he met on board the handsome, highly respectable, and religious lad who was to be his close friend for the next seven years, Joseph Bernard; and as the ship sailed on from Gibraltar to Algiers, Syracuse, Smyrna, Port-Said, Malta, Oran, Tenerife, and across to Bahia, New York and Halifax, Loti became more accustomed to life at sea and the fun to be had in foreign ports of call, particularly in Algiers, where they could lose themselves in the casbah, and New York where they arrived in time to enjoy the Independence Day celebrations.

On their return to France, the trainees of the "Jean Bart" learn that the Franco-German War has begun and, after being rapidly put through their exams, are transferred to other vessels involved in various theaters of the war. Loti is embarked on the corvette "Decrès" a week after returning to port, in August, 1870, and for the next eight months participates in "what was in fact an open game of hide and seek"[10] which the French boat plays with the Prussian navy as part of its blockade in Heligoland and the Baltic. The weather is cold and windy, the scenery is bleak, and the "Decrès" is under constant bombardment from Prussian ships such as the "König Wilhelm." Clearly, apart from landing at Copenhagen and exploring some of the Danish outer isles, Loti did not enjoy this particular episode in his naval beginnings; it was too static and lacking in color for him; it was the harsh reality he later described in *Pêcheur d'Islande* and not the tropical exoticism he dreamed of. He was pleased therefore when the war ended with Sédan and he joined the dispatch boat "Vaudreuil" which, after a brief cruise down the French coast during the events of the Commune in Paris, set sail in May, 1871, for South America and the Pacific.

En route, the ship stopped in Brazil and Loti was encouraged to go on a hunting expedition in the jungle; he was so appalled by the killing of monkeys and birds, which he later described in the tale

Mes Dernières Chasses, that he vowed never to repeat the experience. Loti lands at Valparaiso in October, 1871; here, like Gustave before him, he meets a Chilean woman who tries to teach him some national dances in her garden in Almendral—an incident he recalled in *Passage de Carmencita*—and here too he is told, as he recalled in *Un Jeune Officier Pauvre,* to move from the "Vaudreuil," "where I was so uncomfortable to embark on the fine frigate, the "Flore," and sail at last to Tahiti, to have what I had dreamed of throughout my childhood come true."

IV *The Midshipman Artist*

Before proceeding to Tahiti, the "Flore" stopped during the first week of 1872 at Easter Island at the request of the French government in order to explore it and bring back one of the huge monoliths for the Jardin des Plantes museum in Paris; the ship was also to call at the Marquesas Islands and other small isles before anchoring off Papeete at the end of January, 1872. It was for the better understanding of the sketches Loti did on this voyage and later had published in France that he began formally to write down his impressions of what he saw and found overseas.

Loti had inherited from his parents a certain artistic talent and had always enjoyed drawing in his childhood; his sister Marie, who had studied art under Louis Cognet in Paris and had enjoyed on her return to Rochefort painting the people and plants around her, encouraged this trait in her small brother by her example and tuition. Thus, when Loti goes to Paris, he follows in her footsteps on his visits to the Louvre and also wants to copy the pictures he sees; he writes to her in October, 1866: "One can imagine oneself being an artist when one is surrounded by all these magnificent pictures; I felt that I too should paint."[11] When he embarks on the "Borda", he regrets he has not his paintbox with him so that he could paint the Breton countryside; one of his teachers on board allows him, however, to sketch during class and places his room at his disposal for his painting when his paintbox arrives. On the "Jean Bart" Loti continues to do quick sketches of the ports they visit; hence the perspicacious commander's comment on him at the end of the voyage as "a rather spoilt child with a weak constitution and without any aptitude for life at sea, an artist by

nature."[12] On the "Vaudreuil" and the "Flore," too, Loti did his
sketches of the savages of Cape Horn and the desolate landscape
of the Straits of Magellan, of the sorcerers and tribesmen of
Dakar, and of the monoliths and tattooed natives of the Pacific
islands. It is from his sister that Loti inherits his fine detail and
sensitivity to shape and color, reflected not only in his art, but in
their common interest in plants and insects, and it is for her that,
initially, he draws his porthole on the "Borda" and his close friend
on board, Lucien-Hervé Jousselin, a valley on Las Palmas, and his
cabin on the "Flore."

Similarly, apart from the short *journal de route* he kept during
the training coastal cruise on the "Bougainville" in August, 1868,[13]
it is initially for his own satisfaction and for Marie that he begins to
write down his impressions to supplement the sketches in prose;
he had already expressed to her a vague wish to write in a letter
of 5 January 1869[14] among many other romantic projects. His impressions of his early experiences at sea can be found in his letters
to Marie and, slightly revised at a later date, in *Un Jeune Officier
Pauvre*. The Viaud family talents for writing and drawing became
interrelated in Loti owing to his initial desire to convey to those at
home a complete impression of what he himself was then experi-
encing, just as he was trying to do for himself in his *journal intime*.
Hence, shortly after he sends the first batch of pictures of South
America and the Pacific to Marie in May, 1872, from San Fran-
cisco, he also forwards her extracts from his *journal intime* to
supplement his art with some cohesive explanation and personal
impressions; and it was thus not only very fine drawings of the
tattooed natives and monoliths that Marie had published in August
1872, and September–October, 1873, in *L'Illustration* with the help
of Loti's aunt Nelly Lieutier-Besson, but also the young *sous-
officier's* notes on, and impressions of, these. No picture could convey the mystery of the natives of Rapa Nui's origins and isolation,
the strangeness of their culture, or their childish attitude to the
French crew in search of souvenirs; no sketch could bring the color
and action of the scene so alive. Take for example this description
of the young boy, Petero, who jumps aboard:

Oh, what an amazing, thin face he had, with a little hooked nose and eyes
that were too close together and too large and looked both wild and

sad! He is quite naked, very thin and muscular, his whole body alert; his skin is a reddish copper color and decorated with fine blue tattooings; his hair, also dyed red, is tied at the back of his head with a number of scabious stalks, which give him a flamelike crest as they rise in the breeze. He gazes at us with his wide-open eyes full of fear and wonder. There is in him something of the fascination of an imp or goblin.[15]

Or these impressions of the giant monoliths on the farther side of the island at the foot of Ranoraraku crater:

They do not resemble at all, in fact, those which were lying down, strewn by the dozen across our path. Although they appear to be from a more remote period, they are the work of much less simple artists; they bear an expression and inspire fear. Moreover, they are without a body and have only colossal heads rising up out of the ground on the end of long necks and standing aloft as if to scan the eternally empty, motionless horizons.

Always, the concentration of concise yet imaginative personal impressions and simple, comprehensive style of the Viaud family's intense correspondence predominates in Loti's accounts. The fact that most of the material Loti wrote on the Marquesas island of Nuka-Hiva was later inserted in Part II of *Le Mariage de Loti* shows not only how much his literature owed to reality, but how far Loti had already gone along the road to his literary success of some six years later; an approach and a style had already evolved; all that was needed was the inspiration of a story; and that Tahiti was to provide.

CHAPTER 2

The Exotic Pierre Loti

I Le Mariage de Loti

A LTHOUGH the critic Ferdinand Brunetière[1] scoffed somewhat at the exoticism of Loti's first three novels and the similarity of their plots, no just assessment of Loti's development and accomplishment could be made without considering them; for they record not only Julien Viaud's early life in the navy and his travels from 1872 to 1877 in Tahiti, Senegal and Turkey, but reveal the blossoming of those artistic and literary talents which were to give birth to the genius of Pierre Loti.

Although *Le Mariage de Loti* was not Loti's first published novel—this privilege belonging to *Aziyadé*—it is one of his first works and the one most concerned with the earliest of his naval adventures: those in Polynesia. It was composed in late 1878 and early 1879, partly during Loti's stay at Cherbourg in between coastal maneuvers on the "Moselle," and accepted by the publishers of *Aziyadé,* Calmann-Lévy, with whom Loti had signed a six-year contract in March, 1878. At the same time, Mme Juliette Adam, who later claimed she had "discovered" Loti's talent[2] and was henceforth to become the novelist's "intellectual mother,"[3] published the work in serial form in the January and February, 1880, issues of the *Nouvelle Revue,* which she had founded the previous month. *Rarahu* or *Le Mariage de Loti,* as it came to be called, thus appeared anonymously, dedicated to the actress Sarah Bernhardt whose influential indulgence the obscure author of *Aziyadé* humbly craved, exactly a year after Loti's first novel; and although Mme Adam's claim to have discovered Loti might be disputed, since this honor clearly belongs to Calmann-Lévy and it is known that Mme Adam at first nearly declined *Rarahu,* it must be mentioned to her credit that her influence with writers like Daudet and Goncourt and the novel's serialization in the review did largely contribute to the emergence of Loti's success in France.

Le Mariage de Loti was, like all Loti's later novels, written well after the events described and contains that highly sentimental, personal mixture of realism and romanticism associated with his work. Just as the young dreamer of La Limoise and Oleron had shared his mother's fetishistic sentimentalism with regard to any absent member of the family circle in his childhood, and had projected the exotic settings of his miniature theater and his reading onto the banal Saintonge scenery and life around him, so the older writer tended to elaborate retrospectively in his work on his experience overseas so as to try to overcome the shortcomings of his present reality and his own weaknesses in it. This process was encouraged by the fact that Loti's work was often created from "a realistic experience grafted onto a romantic predisposition,"[4] which was based on a true reality over which a web of the author's personal fantasy had been woven by his knowledge of a country and imaginative evocation of it long before he visited it. In the case of *Le Mariage de Loti,* his realism is based on his stay of seventy-three days on Tahiti—not nearly two years as in the novel— from 19 January to 23 March and 26 June to 4 July 1872, and the impressions he noted down in his *journal intime* and the articles that appeared in *L'Illustration* in August, 1872, and September-October, 1873. His details of life, language, customs, and beliefs in the novel were then collected on the spot, apart from the sparse information on the history of the islands he gleaned from the admiral of the "Flore's" library. His account of Queen Vaekehu's agony can be found in a letter he sent to Marie in January, 1872. Even the letters quoted in Tahitian in the novel were based on some received by a naval surgeon, Nadaud, from two native girls, Topire and Rerao.[5]

The romantic element that allowed Loti to escape his wintry surroundings and ascetic life in Cherbourg during the novel's composition and provides its plot was itself derived from reality; it is based on Loti's brother Gustave's relationship with a Tahitian girl named Tarahu in 1859–1861;[6] Loti has simply altered Tarahu to Rarahu for his love plot and given Tarahu's role in the novel to Taïmaha just as he has changed the names of Gustave's Tahitian offspring from Taüvira and Puta to Atario and Taamari; in short, disguising the real names and making his hero British instead of French, and basing his description of his Tahitian heroine on girls he met during his stay and on his own experiences with Joseph

Bernard on the island,[7] Loti has personalized his brother's experiences in the novel and also idyllicized them. This was due to
Loti's exotic dreams of Tahiti in his childhood and the sentimental
cult Loti, Marie, and the Viaud family had devoted to Gustave
while he was away from home and more especially after his death
in 1865; Marie's attempt at novel writing, *Autour de Paulette*,
based on a sailor's quest for links with his family in the Pacific islands, derived from this cult and anticipated Loti's work. It was
natural that Loti, now he had the opportunity he had desired so
long of visiting Tahiti and seemed to be following in Gustave's
footsteps, should try and find out about his brother's life there.
While stopping off in Guyana, he had already sought for memories
of his childhood friend Lucie Duplais, who had recently died on
returning to France from living out there, and he wrote to Marie
on 22 October 1871 that he intended enquiring about Gustave's
past in Tahiti once he had established himself with his friend on
the island: "our intention is to rent there a small house to use as
a home for the two of us, but for some time now I have been
thinking that there is probably no trace of Him or His stay still
left; He is no doubt as forgotten there as Lucie was in the Iles du Sa-
lut. . . ."[8]. When, however, his quest for some vestige of Gustave's
memory and more particularly for his Tahitian offspring comes to
nought, Loti reveals in a letter of 18 July 1872 to Marie how ob-
sessive his cult of his brother had become: "For three months I had
got used to the idea of his two children, I was happy in believing in
their existence, which had become vital to me . . ."[9]

If the love plot of the novel, derived from this cult of Gustave,
provided necessarily a personally romanticized and idyllicized view
of Tahitian life, its fragmentary structure of short sketches, letters,
and *journal intime* descriptions serve to counter this by their impression of realism. *Le Mariage de Loti* is nothing if not Polynesia
seen through the clear, dreamy eyes Loti inherited from his mother
and shared with his sister, a retrospective superimposing of a pre-
conceived romantic sentimentalism on a precise yet simple foundation in reality that has made one critic of Loti refer to the novel as
a collection of "precise details in a vague framework."[10]

The main story of the novel is simply the temporary "marriage"
of midshipman Harry Grant to a Tahitian girl from Bora Bora,
Rarahu, during the visit of his ship, the "Reindeer," to Papeete;

the marriage, contracted in the first pages of the novel, in which Grant is given the name Loti, is merely the means for his insights into Tahitian life and his comparisons of it with Europe. He paints for us the courts of Queen Pomaré at Papeete and Queen Vaekehu on Nuka Hiva, he gives details of the Maori religion and its language, he refers to the customs of some of the natives such as the old man who sells his beard to a neighboring island, he quotes local songs, legends and dialogue, and describes events such as the return of the fishermen at Papara and the consecration of a temple at Afareahitu. It is, however, through his relations with the figure of Rarahu herself that Loti shows what Tahiti meant to him; the subplot of his search for his brother's mistress Taïmaha and two children is merely an account of Loti's actual quest for Gustave's past, which completes this personalized recreation of his brother's stay in the rest of the novel; Rarahu thus becomes a symbol of Gustave's Tahiti seen through Loti's eyes by this synthesis of periods and people.

In appearance, Raraku has the dark languorous eyes, the long, perfumed hair and the reddish-brown, well-proportioned, tattooed body clad in only a loose *pareo* skirt of all the Tahitian girls Loti met. She has their temperament too; splashing around in the Fataoua stream with her friend Tiahoui or sitting on its banks singing or dreaming, she epitomizes for Loti the idyllic calm and naturalness of this island inhabited by a mysterious race and lost in the expanse of the Pacific. Her idyllic simplicity, indicated by her naïve Tahitian dialogue, her primitive fear of nocturnal spirits, and her childish behavior of smiles, tears and fits of temper, matches the natural sensuality of her naked, languorous body as she lazes beside the stream, reflected in Loti's description of the richly perfumed setting and reminiscent of Gauguin's paintings:

The air was heavy with rich tropical aromas, particularly the strong perfume of the oranges on the trees becoming overripe in the midday sun. Nothing broke that utter silence of the midday hour in the Pacific islands. Reassured by our stillness, small lizards, blue like turquoise, moved about us, while black butterflies with markings of large violet eyes on their wings flitted nearby. All that could be heard was the gentle trickling of water, the muted hum of insects, or now and then the crashing sound of an overripe guava that was crushed as it fell to the ground, flavoring the air with the taste of raspberries. . . .

Loti's marriage to Rarahu brings out the contrast between
Tahitian and European ways of life. Loti already implies this by
juxtaposing what is happening at one end of the globe with events
at the other: for example, Loti's "wedding" takes place at the
hour people in London and Paris are coming out of the theaters;
and he refers to the Fataoua stream running upside down to the
lakes of Hyde Park or the Bois de Boulogne. The contrast is best
seen in Rarahu's naïve ignorance of the poker game she watches
being played at Pomaré's palace and the ease with which the
Tahitians are taken in by the Chinese sweetsellers; it is also
emphasized by Loti's observations on the lazy life of the islanders:

> The years pass for the Tahitians in complete idleness and perpetual
> reverie—and these childish adults do not even suspect that in our wonder-
> ful Europe so many poor souls are killing themselves trying to earn their
> daily bread. . . .

It is finally stressed by Rarahu's fate during and after her blissful,
frivolous life with Loti in the little house in Papeete surrounded by
a copse of coconut palms and decorated with hibiscus, mimosa and
periwinkle, where she entertains both Pomaré's court and the
"Reindeer's" crew. For while the sophisticated European in Loti
is fascinated by the simple and contemplative nature of Rarahu,
which he himself possessed in his childhood, and enjoys the warmth
of her naïve affections, she begins to lose her savage innocence and be
corrupted by contact with civilization; their installation in the little
cottage at Papeete and their entertaining is the first step in her
decline.

Through her contact with Loti, she comes to distinguish how she
can please him by her clothes and her manner; from living in the
town, she becomes paler and develops a bronchial condition; her
life with Loti and her intercourse in Papeete confuse the morality
she has imbibed from her Bible; she soon becomes jealous of the
Europeanized princesses of Pomaré's court and starts to speak some
English to please her master. Rarahu's corruption is symbolic of
the fate of Tahiti as a whole; for Tahiti, too, is declining. Queen
Pomaré stoically watches the corrupting effects of European
civilization on her kingdom: the loss of native habits and culture,
the spread of prostitution and disease, the decline of her family. The
death of Pomaré's daughter and the agony of the Queen herself

almost coincide with the decline and end of Rarahu, recounted through Loti's conversations with naval officers who have visited the island since his own departure, and his disillusionment with his brother's mistress Taïmaha, whose children were from her affair with another man. If Loti's playing of Meyerbeer at the last of Pomaré's parties and the young princess' release of the wild birds Loti had given her anticipate these events, the fading flower Rarahu refers to in her poetic letters to Loti and the pressed blooms he takes from his luggage on his arrival home symbolize the passing away of Rarahu and all that she and Tahiti meant for him. Nothing remains of their love; he had foreseen their separation and was conscious of the differences between them even in the midst of his happiness; his disillusionment at Taïmaha's deception and Rarahu's fall merely confirms the ephemeral nature of his Tahitian idyll and the death of Maori life. As the novel's epigraph of a Tahitian saying implies, men may die but Nature alone persists; the stream at Fataoua and the forests and mountains of Tahiti survive and flourish while the Maori race and their culture die away; and with them Loti's version of an idyllic paradise before its fall at the hands of civilization.

II   Le Roman d'un Spahi

As Loti sailed back to Europe from the Pacific, he thought he was going to have a long period of leave at home to see his family; but this was not to be. On reaching Brest, he was ordered straightaway to Toulon and from 10 December 1872 to 9 January 1873 put on the payroll of the frigate "Provençale." He then went on coastal maneuvers between Toulon and Villefranche on the "Savoie" for the next three months. At the end of these he was, however, granted three months' shore leave and made straight for Rochefort to see his mother and aunts. On 26 June he was promoted sub-lieutenant and, hearing that his close friend on the "Flore," Joseph Bernard, was being sent to Senegal, decided to seek the help of Joseph's uncle, M. de Ségur, in gaining priority over other officers being posted in West Africa. He wrote to Marie at this stage: "This is the country that Joseph and I like most apart from Oceania and it would be marvelous for both of us if this voyage came off. And since my immediate situation is not yet

determined ... we might as well go together."[11] The matter was
soon arranged and Loti embarked as a passenger on the "Entre-
prenante" bound for Dakar on 1 September 1873. Here he established himself in a thatched hut complete with marabou stork,
monkey and parakeet as pets. From November, 1873, to May,
1874, Loti cruised back and forth on the "Pétrel" between Dakar
and Saint-Louis and visited some remote areas at the mouths of
the Mellacorée and Minez rivers, described in *Un Jeune Officier
Pauvre*. Back in Saint-Louis in January, Loti complains to Marie
of the monotony of the gay, busy life he is leading;[12] apart from
some odd sketches of the King of Dakar, Mahomed Diop, of the
Tuareg tribesmen with whom he rides out into the Sahara, and of
the native life around him, he has little time for drawing or
writing. Furthermore, the feverish heat makes any strenuous work
impossible in this dull colonial town.

Two events broke the tedium of Loti's existence there, however:
The first was a brief romance with a creole girl, Coumba Felicia; the
second was his attraction to the wife of a French merchant of
Dakar in April–May, 1874. This latter romance caused a turmoil
in Loti's life for not only was the lady concerned already married,
but she abandoned him and sailed for Europe in June. Loti was
apparently heartbroken and, as he later recounted in *Un Jeune
Officier Pauvre,* on his return to France in October, 1874, he
sought to see her at her home near Geneva. Indeed, as late as
1878–1879, Loti still refers to the failure of this romance and
although Loti later destroyed many of the notes he made during
this time, it is clear that, whether the romance was as passionate
in reality as he implied later or not,[13] Senegal and Saint-Louis were
to remain in his mind as "that part of Africa where I so deeply
loved and so deeply suffered".

Loti returned, full of anguish, to France in September, 1874,
on board the "Espadon." As in the case of *Le Mariage de Loti,
Le Roman d'un Spahi* was not written until some years after Loti's
experiences: in June, 1880, at Toulon in fact. Loti wrote most of
it within a month though with some difficulty due to the painful
memories it evoked, and told Mme Adam in October, 1880, "I
will probably never write anything more powerful than this
book".[14] His friend Jousselin corrected his script[15] and the novel
appeared anonymously like the other early works in the *Nouvelle*

Revue from 15 March to 15 May 1881. When Calmann-Lévy published it in volume form in the following September, however, it was signed Pierre Loti—the first of his novels to be so.

The novel describes the experiences of the handsome, scarlet-cloaked spahee Jean Peyral—"a superb example of noble charm and virile perfection"—during his four years in the French colonial town of Saint-Louis; these include his short-lived affair with a creole beauty from Paris, Cora, who encourages his advances and then cruelly deceives him, and his relationship with a fifteen-year-old Khassonké girl in Cora's service, Fatou-gaye, whose native charms lead him to forsake his family and fiancée in France and who later bears his child before he is killed in some intertribal fighting. As in *Le Mariage de Loti,* the setting is based on reality; his descriptions of the people collecting the fish jumping out of the sea, of the natives' hair styling, of the women pounding grain in the Yolof villages, of the local musicians and dances for the festive *bamboulas,* of the tribal superstitions and dependence on the magic powers of different bracelets, and of places like the marketplace of Guet-n'dar and the river route to Podor are as clear and detailed as those of Tahiti; their artistic rendering can be seen in the sketches of Senegal that Loti had published in *L'Illustration* and *Le Monde Illustré.*[16] The events in the novel are also related to those in Loti's own life: The affair with Cora is a fusion of those of Loti with Coumba Felicia and the European woman; Peyral's boredom and loneliness were Loti's in Saint-Louis; his longing for home was also Loti's; Peyral's character derived from spahees Loti met—Loti mentions in *Un Jeune Officier Pauvre* meeting a "Jean Peyral" on the "Espadon" and remarks elsewhere that "Peyral" was one of the few survivors of their stay in Senegal[17]—and the idea of his liaison with Fatou and her child was probably a vestige of the quest for Gustave's offspring in Tahiti.[18] Nevertheless, if the setting and framework of the plot are again founded on reality, the mood of desire and death of the novel is, as in *Le Mariage de Loti,* inspired by Loti's romanticized memories of his own love and anguish.

When Peyral arrives in Saint-Louis, it is September and the beginning of the Senegalese dry season; all is dry and as if fossilized by the torrid heat; a deathly stillness hangs over everything and the only sign of life comes from the vultures lying in wait in the feverish atmosphere on the mastodon-like baobab trees. Saint-Louis itself is still and silent like a cemetery; its whitewashed houses cover it like a shroud; vultures circle overhead and jackals prowl on its outskirts; it has the air of a "once flourishing colonial outpost that is now dying," isolated as it is by breakers from the sea and virtually surrounded by stagnant marshes and parched desert. In such a tedious *milieu* it is only natural that Peyral, with his "grave, male beauty" and "stature to play the lover's role in a romantic melodrama," should feel lonely and be taken in by the wiles of the elegant but blasé Cora. It is significant, however, that his affair with a sophisticated European should come to such a swift and tragic end in so wild and fatal a place owing to her cynical deception of him and should lead him to drink, debauchery, and attempting to commit suicide; for it is this failure with a representative figure of European values that brings him into an ever closer relationship with the simple, young, and naked Fatou-gaye of Sudanese stock and into fatal contact with the sensual delights of black Africa.

Fatou-gaye epitomizes the primitive, animal instincts and agile strength of the simple and superstitious African, be they the gorilla-like rowers he sees on arriving at Saint-Louis or the intensely lively dancers of Coura-n'diaye. Appropriately, Peyral's attraction to her coincides with the coming of spring and the revival of vital forces in Nature celebrated in frenzied tribal dancing; his family and fiancée in Europe, his religion and moral scruples of the past, are all sacrificed to the pagan lust and toxic pleasures of darkest Africa. He forgets the sinister signs of death around him that come to the fore again when the baobab loses its parched leaves and becomes once more a timeless skeleton; he forgets the corpses and the vultures, jackals and hyenas he saw in the desert; he fails to recall the atmosphere of fever and death in the hospital at Saint-Louis where he lay suffering a breakdown shortly after Cora's deception; he takes no notice of the black, velvet wings of the bats that glide over himself and Fatou when they meet each night at Sorr; and he is not alerted by the ominous toast to their fallen comrades at the spahees' farewell dinner before his company leaves for France. In short, he does not see that in arranging to stay on in Senegal he is signing a death pact with Africa; he has a vague premonition that he may never see his home and family again, but his complacency and pity with regard to Fatou, who knows exactly how to get round him with her feline childishness and sensual attractiveness, prevent him considering it further. Even when she sells the old watch his father gave him, and the fetishistic sentiment he has for this and for a charm his mother presented him with in childhood prompts him at last to evict her, he finds he cannot do without her for long and is glad to discover her later with his child on the steamer going to Podor and Dialdé, where the spahees have been summoned to help fight against the forces of Boubakar-Ségon; for his fiancée Jeanne Méry's unfortunate marriage to a deformed but wealthy and respectable municipal official reveals to him the sacrifices of fiancée, family, marriage, and promotion he has made and the tomblike hollowness now of his lonely life.

His journey to Dialdé will lead to his final self-sacrifice, already hinted at in the descriptions of the crocodiles lurking on the steamy river banks and in the references to Fatou's superstitious fear of death if she sees a hippopotamus and symbolized in the claustrophobic sweep of the plains around Podor and his fear of being enclosed by the circle of dancing Bambara tribesmen. His death in an ambush is far from heroic or epic; there is no Homeric praise here of his valor; his struggle with a powerful native ends with his being brutally stabbed and gushing blood; his delirious dreams of his mother and home are interrupted by the hungry howling of jackals and his crude despoliation by local villagers; the poison that Fatou-gaye takes and the strangulation of her child complete this lurid setting of his death. He dies the savage, primitive death of the African wilderness surrounded by the black mistress and child who kept him there, at the same time as his former fiancée is getting married in France. The novel's final note is a refrain of pity and cynicism, reminiscent of the macabre in Baudelaire:

Poor mother, poor old woman! . . . That human form, which can just be seen in the shadows, which is lying there in such isolation with its mouth gaping toward the star-studded sky and sleeping now when the beasts of the jungle are ready to prowl, will, alas, never rise to its feet again! Poor mother, poor old woman!—that body left lying there is your son! . . . Tomorrow, enormous, bald-headed vultures will complete Nature's destruction of the soldiers' bodies—their bones will lie on the desert sands,

shared out among the animals, and their skulls will be bleached by the sun
and burrowed into by the wind and the grasshoppers . . . Dear, old parents,
go on awaiting your son, await the return of the spahee!

Loti symphathizes with the old parents of Peyral in the Cévennes,
but he appreciates at the same time the spahee's life and tragic
fate in Senegal as part of Nature's processes in the African wild.
There is also in this epilogue a note of detachment from and revolt
against the moral values of Peyral's Protestant family, which
may perhaps be related to a similar development in Loti's
own life. For although Loti's heart remained constantly with his
mother and family on his voyages overseas, his attachment to their
traditional morality and faith had begun to waver.

III   A Year of Crisis

As early as May, 1867, Loti wrote to Marie from Paris shortly
after his confirmation at the Chapelle du Saint Esprit: "Since then
I have been assailed by doubts and uncertainties . . . The uncer-
tainty I felt two days afterward. . . has increased since my return
to Paris and is grave enough to torment me."[19] The impact of the
natural beauties and native life he saw on his travels and the free,
gay existence he could enjoy as a naval officer as well as the various
tragedies in his early life at home undermined the rigidity of the
faith of his childhood even further. Marie continued, however, to
sermonize her brother in strict Protestant terms and a firm, parental
manner in her letters to him; and he continued to submit all his
confidences to her, aware of his mother's likely displeasure. The
passion with which he surrounded his attraction to the married
woman in Saint-Louis almost undermined his moral scruples and
faith completely, as he later recalled in Un Jeune Officier Pauvre.
Moreover, the coincidental breaking up of his close friendship
with Joseph Bernard filled him with a grave sense of deception and
revolt against all of life.

On his return to Rochefort, he found the old house in contrast to
Senegal irritatingly quiet and dead and resorted to going out
drinking with the local sailors to overcome the anguish and despair he felt. On 25 January 1875 he finally leaves home for Joinville
near Paris to go on a physical training course for seven months,

which, considering his later remark to Mme Adam "I would give anything to possess the beauty I do not have,"[20] has the appearance of being a consolation for his recent lack of success with women as well as a form of escape from a frustrating reality. Such is his despair that he leaves behind his Bible, an action which his mother regards with grave misgivings; she writes to him on 2 February: "I regret what we have lost of you, the change that has come over you —a change on which I am not, alas, the only one to remark. . . ."[21] This sense of defiance and revolt against his family's ways associated with his memories of Senegal was naturally reflected in *Le Roman d'un Spahi;* not only in the description of the brothel Peyral frequents—an episode Loti borrowed from his friend Pierre Le Cor's experiences in Uruguay—and the lust he feels, but also in the brutality of the spahee's death, which almost symbolizes Africa's and Nature's fatal victory over the European and Protestant in him—just as Senegal represented the grim rejection of love and faith in Loti's own development.

IV Aziyadé

As spring, 1876, arrives, Loti's spirits begin to revive after the anguish and depression that followed his experiences in Senegal; in April, while awaiting further orders on board the "Thétis" at Toulon, he even shows the benefits of his physical training course at Joinville by performing as a clown acrobat in a local circus! On 9 May he leaves Hyères on board the armored frigate "Couronne" for Salonica, where the French and German consuls had recently been murdered, and after a short time there from 16 May to 29 July —during which the supposed assassins were executed to the satisfaction of the European powers and the consuls' funeral took place—he sails on to Istanbul, where he stays until 17 March 1877. The whole object of the exercise was to make the French presence felt in the area during the uneasy period following the Bulgarian atrocities. Loti writes to his sister on 29 August 1876 from the "Gladiateur," to which he had been transferred on arrival in Turkey, that he goes horseriding and enjoys sailing and rowing up the Bosphorus: "The role of the "Gladiateur" consists of making a weekly excursion for a day or so along the Asian coast to beauty spots or places known for their historic interest. The idea is to show off the Ambassador, those attached to the Embassy and the lovely ladies who compose their suite."[22] His time in Istanbul is thus quite a pleasant one. He is enraptured by the traditionalism of Turkish life and the faded beauty of Islamic culture; he thus stays at first in the poor quarter of Eski and then moves to the Moslem sector of Eyub; and after quite a lot of bribery, manages to find himself close enough to the Sultan to do some sketches of his barge and coronation for the *Monde Illustré*. He also becomes acquainted with a nineteen-year-old Circassian girl, whom he had seen in Salonica and met again in Istanbul four months after his own arrival there in August, 1876. Her memory was to remain with him up to the hour of his death and their romance was immortalized in Loti's first novel, *Aziyadé*, published by Calmann-Lévy in January, 1879.

Loti claimed at the time in a letter to his friend Lucien Jousselin,[23] who corrected the manuscripts of his early works and had passed on *Aziyadé* to the publisher Michel Lévy, that the novel was merely his memoirs of his stay in Turkey;[24] and Claude Farrère was much later to quote Loti as saying that the story was true and only the names had been altered:[25] Aziyadé's real name had been Hakidjé and the two boys Achmed and Samuel, who acted as servants during Loti's meetings with her in the old house at Eyub, were Mehmed and Daniel; while Loti's Turkish name during his stay there had been Ali Nyssin and not Ari-Effendi as in the novel. Although the authenticity of much of Loti's realism cannot be denied—much of the novel being taken with slight alterations from actual correspondence between himself and his family or Jousselin[26] and the English disguise in which he diplomatically clothes his French characters can, as in *Le Mariage de Loti*, be easily seen through —it seems most unlikely from his letters at the time that his romance was as he later described and viewed it.[27] *Aziyadé* with its allusions to Persian poetry, Musset's Rolla, Hassan, and Portia, Hugo's *Orientales* and *Chants du Crépuscule*, and even Shakespeare's Romeo and Juliet was, like Loti's other early works, a Romantic evocation in retrospect of his real experience of the age-old charm of Turkey's eclipsed splendor, a poetic memory rather than just an occasionally enjoyable reality.

As the subtitle and preface of the novel explain, this is the story as recounted through the notes and letters of an English naval lieutenant who is killed in the service of Turkey in October, 1877.

The young officer arrives in Salonica on the day the consuls' assassins are hanged; here, during his stroll through the quiet streets, he catches sight of a young, yashmaked Circassian girl in a notable's harem; he is so enchanted by her that he arranges to meet her at night in a boat on the coast despite the difficulties this involves and the risks they run. When his ship sails on to Istanbul, she promises to contact him again there when her master will visit Turkey and Asia very shortly. This she does; indeed, she visits Loti each night in his house in the Moslem sector of the city and his solitude and anguish before her arrival are replaced by affection and ecstasy. Unfortunately, he all too soon has to leave her since his ship is returning to England; their heartbreak coincides with the outbreak of war in Turkey. When the young officer returns to Istanbul shortly afterward, he finds the city in ruins and his loved one dead; in memory of her and of her country, he virtually commits suicide by joining the Turkish army in their fight against the Russian invasion.

As in Loti's other works, the Turkish *milieu* is brought alive not only by the use of native words and dialogue, but by the realistic description of local incidents: the dangers of going out at night in the sinister Turkish quarter and impressions of the festivals of Bairam and Surré-humayun, the annual puppet shows, the prostitution and dancing of young boys, and the casual life around the mosques and in the cafés. Here, the young officer, depressed by his experiences of life with its deceptions and spiritual and physical suffering and irritated by the increasing sophistication and egalitarianism of modern Western society, can find both the traditional aristocratic culture of an age-old civilization where little has changed since the coming of Islam and the simple emotions of a devout, primitive people. His description of the square near the Sultan Mehmed-Fatih mosque reflects his love of their traditional ways, beliefs, and costumes:

The Mehmed-Faith square dominates old Istanbul and occupies a vast area where men in kashmir caftans and large white turbans stroll about. The mosque that rises in the middle of it is one of the most vast in Constantinople and also one of the most sacred. . . .

This sector of the city leads a totally Eastern way of life; camels cross it slowly, tinkling all the time their little bells; dervishes come and sit around to discuss religious matters; nothing has reached here yet from the West.

He is aesthetically fascinated by the colorful spectacle of the Sultan's coronation with its hundreds of different costumes and the richly bejeweled furnishings of the Sultan's palace and enjoys indulging in the antique, aristocratic luxury of Izedden Ali-effendi's house with its thick carpets, satin cushions, and gold-coated hookahs. Furthermore, he can enjoy here in Turkey greater freedom than in Western Europe, thanks to his anonymity and the casualness of Turkish life and, dressed as a native, can set up home in the holy part of the city and have the devoted service of two poor boys, the handsome Samuel and the affectionate Achmed: as Ari-Effendi of Eyub, he can chat and smoke narghile with other Turks; passively accept their religious and social customs, discuss the political situation with them in the cafés, and generally enjoy the casual life of simple pleasures of these people, who still retain an unsophisticated, natural spontaneity.

Thus, whether it is the aristocratic luxury of Islamic culture or the natural simplicity of the ordinary people, Turkey allows Loti to escape from himself and Europe in the disguise he dons in "Madame's" café in the Galata district; it provides him with the supreme escape from his moral ennui and spiritual despair in the narcotic pleasures of the aristocrat's harem represented by Aziyadé. The young man, who after Senegal abandons his faith and morality in the letters to his family quoted here, professes his skepticism and ennui to his friend Lucien Jousselin, nicknamed Plumkett, and finally asserts to his fellow officer Léon Baudin, here called William Brown:

There is no God, there is no morality, nothing exists of all that I was taught to respect; there is just an existence that passes and from which one is justified in demanding as much enjoyment as possible while awaiting its terrible end in death . . .

He finds in the dark Circassian girl with the green eyes those same escapist delights which the traditional, unspoilt life of Turkey as a whole offers him. Her obedient role as a sophisticated mistress and the concomitant attention she therefore gives to her appearance and her favors—the care she takes with her nails, her hair and her dress, for example, or the perfumes and henna she uses—can be related to the rich splendor of the Sultanate and notables; while her illiterate naïveté, childish impulsiveness, and superstitious beliefs belong to the simplicity of the people of Turkey, just as do the actions and reactions of Achmed and Samuel. By her silent, mysterious charms, she makes him overcome his days of loneliness and anguish by their nights of love and ecstasy; and she provides him, as do the two servant boys, with a host of trivial incidents such as the purchase of a cat, the throwing away of her sandals, and the entertaining of their neighbors, which involve him more and more in the Turkish way of life. Amid this spiritual and physical escapism, Loti is, however, aware that his romance with Aziyadé must come to an end when his ship sails, that his love for her will pass into the eternity of time symbolized by the age-old call to prayer of his neighbor, the muezzin, and that this inner peace is only a brief respite in his troubled destiny. Her ring may be on his finger and her name tattooed on his chest as if to defy the passing of time and memory, but they both know that their love is, like the coronation and constitution of Sultan Abdul-Hamid in the history of Turkey, "a last moment of splendor" before the fateful course of events and death itself overtakes them.

The shadow of Death hangs over the novel from the very beginning with the hanging of the assassins and the murder of Sultan Mourad. Throughout, Sultan Abdul Hamid's revival of Turkey is alluded to as only ephemeral and Loti's references to the cemeteries and funeral parlors of Eyub and the symbolic owl and black loons that hover about the boat in which he and Aziyadé glide along the Golden Horn imply a similar fate for them. The Persian poem Loti quotes on the passing of spring and the nearness of Death as well as the moralistic incident of the blue tit they watch singing just before a funeral procession passes by emphasize this even more. And if the earlier eclipse of the moon, when the Turks superstitiously shoot at the heavens, and the stormy sky that provides an ominous backcloth to Loti and Aziyadé's last trip on the Golden Horn anticipate the coming of war, Aziyadé's crushing a cup in her hand and her bleeding at the party to celebrate Loti's departure symbolize the tragic fate of herself and her country at the hands of her master and the Great Powers. Furthermore, Loti contrives his conclusion so that the young British officer returns to fight for Turkey and learns of her death amid the ruins of Eyub; and that he hears the clarion call to war as he

40   PIERRE LOTI

visits her grave and is killed soon after in the defense of her country.

This tearful ending, which Loti himself later disliked and had simply added to complete his romance in defiance of the facts—he did not join the Turkish forces despite his desire to do so, expressed in *Un Jeune Officier Pauvre,* and Hakidjé did not die until May, 1880—underlines once more the Romantic *poseur* element in Loti's writing and the escapist cloak of virile heroism and melodrama this imaginative faculty provided for his self-protection in his real life. This effect of his imagination is even more evident when the real situation after the close of the novel is considered. While it is true that Loti became attached to Turkey as a country, kept a dress and bag of Hakidjé in his room for the rest of his life, and revered her memory by describing his visits to her grave at Topkapou in later works, it is also clear from his letter to Plumkett of 21 September 1878 that a year after leaving her his concern for her is as limited as during his stay in Salonica;[28] indeed, even when the Russians had marched on Istanbul in March, 1878, Loti, while concerned for her safety, writes telling her to come to France only if all else fails and she thinks she could adapt to French life.[29] This is far from the gallantry of the novel.

The reality of *Aziyadé* was like the romanticized realism of Loti's other early works, "authentic, in fact exaggeratedly authenticated by you,"[30] as Plumkett said of his friend's intimate but excessively passionate and romantic correspondence and as might be said of Loti's diary too. In short, Loti uses the novel with its foundation in a convincing reality of intimate experience as a narcissistic exercise of his imagination to delude himself as well as to prove to the public he was other than he appeared, just as he would pose, often in some disguise or uniform, for photographs; he created his own cult of himself in his writing, using a retrospective cult of his own experiences and a romanticizing cult of people and places derived from his reading and masochistic personal relations—often prototypes of his family ones—so as to conceal from both himself and others his insecurity and childish real self. He wanted to be as strong and handsome as Gustave, like Samuel and Peyral, because he was so small and timid; he wanted to emulate his big brother like Harry Grant and Ari-Effendi because he was so shy with women—hence the chaste, rather cerebral eroticism of his novels' romances; he wanted to appear passionately in love with women like Aziyadé because all his close friends were naval men and sailors who replaced his mother and sister as his *confidents* overseas; he was attracted to the royalty and nobility pertaining to his characters because of his own poverty and lack of power; he described the life and beliefs of faraway lands because those of Europe and his family were breaking up owing to the oversophistication of Western society, the Viauds' financial position at home, and his own spiritual situation. *Aziyadé* might be notable as Loti's first novel for its colorful and evocative descriptions of his exciting life overseas,[31] but it also implicitly provides a clearer insight into his tragic life at home.

V *Loti's Style*

There is this same mixture of the real and the realistic, the personal and the artificial, truth and illusion, in the style of Loti's work as in his personality. It is evident in his contrived use of the diary form and letters as well as in the way he disguises and distorts names and situations in his plots. It is clear, too, that his claim that he had read hardly any literature was completely misleading; for he had a good knowledge of the Bible, some classics, the Romantics, and some current writers,[32] and although he asserts in *Fleurs d'Ennui* that his work was composed from an indiscriminate accumulation of his overall impressions on his travels, his style is, despite its appearance of being "simple, fluent, almost commonplace,"[33] as complex and rhetorical as that of any of his literary contemporaries and not just a felicitous combination of the right evocative words used with subtle discretion as Giraud thought.[34] For his aim is to convey to his readers with what one critic has seen as "sentimental immodesty"[35] his highly personal impressions of an exotic situation—impressions which, as has been explained above, he did not always experience in the way or place he describes. Just as in his sketches of Easter Island and Tahiti he occasionally distorts the scene or subject before him to heighten the impression of mysteriousness and idyllicism he wishes to convey—he reconstructs the monoliths and idealizes the natives[36]—so he carefully arranges his novels to evoke the sensations and thoughts he desires to communicate. In short, he uses an accurate and discriminating realism to render with greater con-

viction a romanticized exoticism behind which he often hid rather
than reveal his true feelings and the real situation.

The simple but evocative realism of Loti's narrative derives
both from the representative selection of typical incidents he describes and from his impressionistic use of vocabulary, syntax and
sentence structure, and the point of view to convey them. He uses
simple words for easy understanding, often repeating them in
slightly different terms or setting them in apposition for emphasis
and greater continuity; occasionally, he contrasts them with exotic
words or uses an indefinite adjective or phrase in order to achieve
a greater impressionistic effect of strangeness; or includes an
abstract noun instead of an adjective for more emphatic effects
of color. Furthermore, the fact that Loti describes only definite
colors, sounds, and scents means that he only requires simple
vocabulary. The apparent simplicity of his sentences also con-
tributes to his prose's dynamism; this he creates[37] by the usual means
of present and past participles and present and imperfect tenses
for effects of immediacy and action; and of questions, exclamations,
short sentences, and indirect free speech or interior monologue to
give prose the fluent realism of dialogue. More specifically, Loti's
artifices for instilling dynamism and immediacy are the infinitive,
imperative, apostrophe, and verb-form at the beginning of sentences; the series of short sentences to convey quick impressions
of a place or itinerary; and the economical use of dots and dashes
in the text to qualify what precedes with implied comment and
separate details or themes without starting fresh sentences.

Finally, Loti achieves a lifelike realism in his exotic settings
by not merely juxtaposing such contrasting facets of life as the
exotic events he describes and the universal sentiments they provoke,
as the critic Jules Lemaître suggested to explain somehow the
strange appeal of Loti's novels,[38] but by maintaining a constantly
changing point of view in his narration and often setting several
points of view in apposition or using them as antitheses within a
paragraph. This device is seen, for example, in the mixture of description, another character's comment, the narrator's impressions,
narrative, and final comments in the scene where Aziyadé leaves
Loti on Séniha's arrival (*Aziyadé*, III, xlv) or in Aziyadé's first
conversation with Loti (*ibid.*, I, xvii); it is underlined by the continual switching of subjects from the first person to the impersonal

on and other impersonal constructions. The idea is to express the scene as simply as possible by repeating facts in different, qualifying terms for effects of immediacy; and to convey a total, comprehensive impression of the scene from various viewpoints and to dissolve the narrator's part into the detail of the action and background about him. In short, while apparently detaching himself from the narrative by switching the viewpoint and giving the appearance of casual realism thereby, Loti remains in firm control of the impression given since all the views relate to him, his actions, or reactions in some way; this allows the reader, as Mme Adam[39] remarked, to view the scene as if through his own eyes and at the next through Loti's while it is in fact always seen through the narrator's.

This technique is not only underlined by the discriminatory economy of the retrospective diary form Loti uses to show a representative collection of realistic scenes, but also by the contrived yet imperceptible manner he builds up a descriptive passage, using a similar series of switching shots to impose his views of the world he is describing. Whether it is Aziyadé's face, the fishermen of Papara, the ball at Pomaré's palace, or Peyral's night at sea near the Equator, Loti constructs his description by first stating the facts of the situation—the weather, time of year, location, hour of the day, or statement of an object or circumstance—and then concentrating like an artist making a draft sketch on the shape or layout of what he is describing; next, he adds some details such as the color or dress or other minor fact to qualify what precedes and gives some impressions of the sounds, smells, and shades of color of the scene and, finally, links these with his imagined themes and mood; thus, gradually, Aziyadé's eyes are related by the green of their pupils to the sea-green praised by Oriental poets; the return of the Tahitian fishermen merges into a scene from prehistoric times through the shells they blow into; the outline of the mountains, banana clumps, and groups of people against the starry sky in Pomaré's gardens is related to the perfume and silence of Tahitian nights, which dispose one to be enchanted by music and by Meyerbeer's *Africaine* in particular; and the warmth and stillness of the equatorial night on board the silent ship makes Peyral think of the geological creation of the earth. In each case, realistic detail—as intricate as the bejeweled coffee cups pointed out on Loti's visit to the Sultan or the crabs' claws noted by Peyral on the riverbank in

Guinea—and impressionistic relief, like the ecstatic sensations felt
by the Fataoua stream or the grating sound of the hanged men's
nails on the ground at Salonica, contribute to the final impression
associated with the narrator's thought or person that Loti wishes
to convey in the novel: the romantic exoticism of Aziyadé, the
fatal idyllicism of Tahiti, and the fossilized primitiveness of Senegal.
These total impressions are as authentically romanticized by a
sort of poetic inflation as his descriptions of the Tahitian streams
and Guinean jungle are in their exaggeratedly realistic represen-
tativeness of the oceanic paradise and the African wild. They are,
nevertheless, contrasted with European values and customs by the
narrator's frequent comparison of the two; this in turn provides
Loti's views on life in France.

His realism becomes thus a mere stepping-stone for the impressionistic communication of his moral ideas; the external world
becomes, as Paul Bourget pointed out,[40] a passive recipient of
Loti's ideas and sensations; the countries he describes become
largely realistic representations in romanticized exotic terms of
his ideal and anguished thoughts on life; and his characters
become functional representatives of his impressions of their
country and implicit criticisms of Europe and only exist through
these, without any individual psychology and development; they
are merely there to epitomize Loti's impressionistic, implicitly
critical evocation of their exotic settings and yet to conceal the
onmipresent imposition on his reader of the particular sentiments
and moral inferences which the author contrives by his style to
convey. Despite the emphasis on the personal and authentic, there
is thus as much complex detachment in the contrivances of Loti's
style as there was in his exoticism and the egocentric cults that
composed it; the refinement of his style does not lie in the preciosity
of the Goncourts' impressionism or the complexity of Gide's
kaleidoscopic approach, with both of which it has close affinities,
but in the deliberate concision of his apparent simplicity for
evocative and moral effect. Just as years earlier he, like his mother
and sister, had been able to evoke life overseas or Gustave's memory
by their sentimental, imaginative attachment to certain objects and
places and to letters received,[41] so in his novels he not only drew on
his travels to romantically recreate his version of life overseas, disguising the names of his characters for his plot—as his sister did

in her draft novel *Autour de Paulette* and Loti did in real life in referring to close friends—but used the dynamic intimacy and detail of their exotic realism in order to convey his moral ideas on life and the personality, which he wished his readers to recognize as his.

Julien Viaud still existed—his remarkable buying of the old house at Rochefort with the help of Henry Duplais and Joseph Bernard in 1871, his unfailing financial support of his mother and aunts, and his treating his mother in Paris in 1881 from the profits of his works prove this —but it was already as Pierre Loti that he was becoming known to such celebrities as Daudet, Goncourt, Feuillet, and Sarah Bernhardt and to the French public of the early 1880s; and this is exactly what he desired, for the image of Pierre Loti in Paris was a projection of the imagination of Julien Viaud in Rochefort.

CHAPTER 3

A Friend of "Brother Yves"

I Loti's Anguish

THE twofold nature of Loti's personality revealed by the discrepancy between the romantic narrator of the early novels and the timid naval officer who wrote them is underlined by the fact that these "exotic" works date from the period after his return from Turkey in late April, 1877, and prior to his first voyage to the Far East in June, 1883, when he was mostly at home or in home waters. From 5 June to 10 August 1877 he is stationary at Rochefort on the "Bouvet"; from 20 September 1877 to 17 June 1878 he is at or around Lorient on the "Tonnerre"; and from September, 1878, to September, 1879, he cruises along the Normandy and Brittany coast on the "Moselle." It is only after a further spell at home and at the Caserne Saint Maurice that he embarks on the "Friedland" at Toulon in April, 1880, and in between cruises along the French coast carries out naval exercises in the Mediterranean, stopping at Algiers, Oran, Tunis, and Bône in April–May, 1880, and again in February, 1881, and taking part in the international patrol of the Yugoslav coast from 9 September to 3 December 1880 following the Dulcingo incident in the conflict between Turkey and Montenegro. And when he disembarks from the "Friedland" as a lieutenant on 24 February 1881, there follows yet another period of little activity on the "Surveillante" at Cherbourg for five months and then he is engaged at the naval headquarters at Rochefort from January to late May, 1883, that is, until he sets out for Indo-China.

As was seen in the last chapter, these years witnessed Loti's success as a writer; he clears the debts incurred on behalf of his family in May, 1880, and the family house at Rochefort is free of its lodgers by October, 1884; he is fêted by Mme Adam in March, 1880, and becomes a close friend of Daudet thereafter, corresponding with him and sending him the draft of his novels; he is known to thousands and a welcome visitor to the elegant salons of Mme Blanche Lee Childe, the Duchesse de Richelieu, and Sarah Bernhardt, in whose exotic apartment he is reputed to have first arrived wrapped in a carpet like Cleopatra before Caesar. In short, he is during these years based at home and out of danger, he is financially secure, and he is famous in all of France. And yet the same discrepancy between Julien Viaud and Pierre Loti seen in the writing of his novels, the same discordant combination of simple emotion and sophisticated desire, of personal authenticity and artistic detachment, as was found in their exotic realism, and an anguished conflict of pantheistic appreciation and nihilistic denigration of life similar to that of his early heroes can be traced in Loti's private existence at this time.

He loves his mother and aunts; he enjoys reading to his Aunt Lalie (Rosalie) who is bedridden and soon to die in April, 1880; he delights in the peace and quiet of the old house with its memories of childhood; he likes being near his sister and niece Ninette at Marennes; and prizes above all being able to walk in the countryside and visit the isle of Oleron, which he does on 14 July 1880 and 2-4 June 1884. But despite all this, he confesses on his thirtieth birthday he is bored and fears the passing of time and growing old; he exclaims when he leaves the "Friedland" in February, 1881, that "everything has grown pale around me and in me all is extinguished";[1] and tells his writer friend and delicate *confident* Emile Pouvillon, who invites him to his house at Montauban in October, 1881, and November, 1884, that he is so desperately lonely and unloved that he sees himself having recourse to prostitutes and then committing suicide;[2] indeed, he confides to Mme Adam that without her friendship and support he could barely carry on.[3] Similar crises of anguish and despair had occurred after his experiences in Senegal and Turkey in late 1874 and January, 1879, when Loti took refuge in a Trappist monastery at Briquebeck near Lorient, but only to leave the following month disillusioned and threatening to poison himself. His only escape, when he was not actually overseas, was his writing of the past and the exotic; in this way, as Loti himself saw, he could occasionally have some respite from his torment like Sisyphus after rolling his rock a little farther up the slope.

For Loti's problem was not easily curable; the traditional stability of faith, hearth, and family was no longer able to support him after the disillusioning effects of the death of his brother and his childhood sweetheart, and the family's bankruptcy: the desires and deceptions of the outside world had severed his spiritual and moral links with the past; the real world of the senses, of nature and evolution, the frailty of the human condition and inevitable coming of death had shattered them. The aesthetic and intellectual development of his sensibility and mind during his experiences overseas increased at once his childhood love of evocative natural things and made his pessimistic understanding of life's processes more sophisticated so that he became both pantheist and nihilist, both indulging in his child's imagination and feeling detached intellectually from it. His timid, withdrawn personality fostered this intellectual development; it was, however, through looking at familiar aspects of life, particularly his life at home, from new points of view that he became aware of the conflict within him; and it was when one of the conflicting selves failed him in life that he sought the other and a spiritual and moral crisis arose out of the clash between the skeptical, almost nihilistic views of the sophisticated man he was fast becoming and the simple values and feelings of his childhood relationship with his family, to which he clung for support.

But he had grown up now, he had read more, his outlook had broadened and his view had become more refined; his profounder knowledge of life's processes, his skeptical attitude to the world and society's values, and the intellectual detachment of his adult aesthetic sensibility were at bottom the overripe fruits of the glut of disillusioning experiences he had had after the dreamy romanticism of his childhood; for life, particularly in the increasingly democratic and soullessly commercialized climate of post-1870 France, could not provide him with the idealism of his child's imagination and forced him like his contemporaries to find compensation in the greater artistic concentration and intellectual refinement of his work; nor could it retain him physically in the childhood emotional relationship with his family to which he clung. His desire for a simple life in France was thus as mythical as his dreams of an exotic romance; it represented the vain and self-conscious attempt of the civilized adult to revert to Nature and his childhood and replace his refined consciousness and aesthetic detachment by his former naïve spontaneity; the mere effort was as self-conscious and dilettantist as the imagination devising it. It can be seen in his concern in his early works with the preservation of his own recent past and the lives and beliefs of simple spontaneous peoples overseas. It is also at the basis of his relations with the lively groups of carousing Breton sailors such as Le Scouarnec and Barrada, with whom he associated in defiance of his family's disdain; of his admiration for their natural vitality and youthful handsomeness in contrast to what he considered his own ageing and physical shortcomings, which he saw as the results of intellectual fatigue and an overcivilized society and tried to compensate for by developing his muscular agility; and of his friendship for Pierre Le Cor, whom he named with affectionate admiration *frère Yves*. A summary of Loti's outlook is provided by his letter to Mme Adam of 5 April 1882:

> At the moment I am given to a sort of vague, melancholy pantheism. I love above all the sun and the solitude of the forests, where I can completely relax and forget everything. I am beginning to understand Nature in a more profound, mysterious, disturbing way. I give myself up to Her. And in so doing I have the greatest horror of all that is related to progress, modern things and ideas, social responsibility, and national solidarity; and a cult of retrospection into the past and all connected with it. . . . How I would like to be like my simple friends from Brittany who grow up and bear their fruit like healthy plants and then die calmly when it is time.[4]

Loti described his inner conflict in *Fleurs d'Ennui* and paid tribute to the simple life of the Bretons in *Mon Frère Yves* and *Pêcheur d'Islande*.

II   Fleurs d'Ennui

The novel, published in the *Nouvelle Revue* in May–June, 1882,[5] takes the form of a dialogue between Loti and his friend Plumkett, both of whom are suffering from their ennui of life; but while Plumkett's spleen is expressed in his skeptical toying with the mysteries of the Beyond and Man's fate in the early religions of the world and given allegorical form in his realistic tale of his travels as the Wandering Jew through China in search of the Son of Heaven, Loti's *ennui* is conveyed by a series of stories and incidents that reveal his distaste for the intellectual sophistication which has contributed to his and Plumkett's disillusionment with life and his desire to retrieve the edifying outlook of an earlier simplicity and faith.

In the allegorical account of the first incident, his dream of the collapse of the old Breton belltower at Creizker while he and Yves are sitting on it and their reappearance as dead men wrapped in primitive wolf skins in a primeval universe, Loti indicates already his fear of the destruction of the age-old, simple life by the fatal coming of sophisticated civilization and his nostalgia for the pre-Adamite naturalness of Creation. It is with this same longing for the uncivilized and simple naturalness of the primeval world that Loti shortly afterwards recalls sighting whales innocently approaching his ship in the rolling seas off the Malouine Islands and evoking for him a scene in the Silurian period of evolution. This natural simplicity Loti finds in Yves, for as Plumkett remarks to him, the Breton sailor represents "the primitive prehistoric savage deep down in yourself"; and it is in the simple life of Brittany that Loti, as he tells Plumkett, felt once again the religious impulses he had experienced intensely during his childhood visits to Oleron. Childhood has passed, however, with its simple ideals and dreams; the days when the accounts register for 1695 of one of his ancestors which he discovered during his childhood could evoke the traditional life of the family for him are as faded by time as the pressed flowers and butterflies in its pages and inspire him with as much spiritual nostalgia as his memories of what Oleron had once meant for him.

This theme of Loti's departure from his spiritual roots in his childhood's natural naïveté and the nostalgia he now feels for them is treated in his series of recollections of the various stages in his life at which he recalls seeing bats; from when he leaned with innocent expectation over the garden wall to see the flowers and butterflies of his first summer and enjoyed the delights of Limoise to when he first seeks the favors of a woman in Paris and, even later, when in Guinea he sees a native kill a bat thought to be the soul of the dead trader Père Barez; from being a free animal flying over the garden on warm summer evenings, the bat evolves in Loti's recollections into the dead creature bottled and labeled *Père Barez's soul* in his study; it thus symbolizes Loti's own evolution from naïve child to sophisticated man and the abandonment of his simple soul in his later life overseas.

The same theme is related in the tale, *Trois Dames de la Kasbah,* which was partly inspired by Loti's visit to Algiers in late April, 1880, when he met two charming Arab girls and their mother but was dismayed, as he told Daudet, at the vice and Westernization that had transformed the city since his previous visit as a cadet. In the tale, three Breton sailors including Yves and three Basque ratings land at Algiers and become lost in the winding, narrow streets of the Casbah; as they fumble their way out of the maze of turnings, they catch sight of three Arab women dressed in their finery waiting silently on the balcony of their house and the three Basques are attracted inside by the smiles of one of the girls; the Bretons, devout and superstitious, stay behind and continue wandering the streets until they enter a bar, become drunk, and steal a cart used for collecting stray dogs in order to reach the harbor. The next morning, both parties meet up on the beach—the Bretons still dazed from their drinking and the Basques just recovering from their night of pleasure—and are arrested and punished as they embark on their ship; the Basques more harshly than the Bretons since they contract and pass on to their simple communities the fatal venereal disease of their Algerian hostesses. The message of the tale is clear: The three Arab women, who are destitute because of their master's death, are "daughters of a condemned race submitting to their fate with mournful resignation"; they epitomize the fallen state of Algiers under cosmopolitan influence; the simplicity and traditional values of their Arab culture have been eroded and corrupted by Western influence just as they in turn pass on the vicious disease of decadent civilization to other simple folk in France.

Loti's short story "Suleïma," in the same volume as *Fleurs d'Ennui,* was similarly inspired by his visits to Oran in April and May, 1880, and his meeting a young Arab girl who reminded him of Hakidjé; Suleïma, like Algiers itself, attracts him when he first sees her by that traditional Arab beauty he liked so much in Istanbul; she is simple and natural like the tortoise he finds at that time and names after her. But unlike the tortoise which survives unchanged the passing of the years, she is corrupted by prostitution in the meantime and when Loti sees her again the beautiful sandalseller's daughter has become a vicious murderess being tried for poisoning her lovers. The fate of both Suleïma and the three women of Algiers can be related to Loti's own view of himself as corrupted by the vices of civilization in the form of the current literary stress on intellectual and aesthetic sophistication.

In the same way, the goatherd heroine of his tale on his acquain-

tance with Mattea Lanovitch and his experiences in Montenegro
and Herzegovina, *Pasquala Ivanovitch,* with her "peasant girl
innocence," is as natural in her love and erotic beauty as the myrtle
and olive groves that witness their romance and the mountain
forests where she tends her flocks; she epitomizes in her devout
simplicity that natural vitality and spiritual integrity Loti admired
in Brittany and Oleron. Unfortunately, the romance must come
to a hasty conclusion when Loti's ship leaves Cattaro; as the autumn
leaves fall from the trees and mists veil the mountain pastures, Loti
addresses to Pasquala his kiss of farewell; the autumnal flowering
of her simple love provides but a brief insight into a world as yet
not too tainted by the sophisticated veneer of civilization, a respite
in the flowering of the withered blooms of Loti's *ennui.* Indeed, the
Fleurs d'Ennui volume closes with Plumkett dissolving his intellectual cares and spiritual anguish in marriage, while Loti is left
alone again amid the debris of his orgy of life's experiences "to roam
the world filled with ennui" and seek a solution to it elsewhere.

III   Mon Frère Yves

Loti found an escape from the sophisticated world of Paris and
the dilettantist refinements of contemporary literature in his friendship with the Breton sailor Pierre Le Cor. Although the latter, who
was nearly a year and a half younger than Loti, had also been on the
"Borda" in 1868–1869, they did not meet until 1877 on the "Tonnerre,'
when they went around everywhere together. Their careers in the navy
were often, however, to diverge after this initial contact and Le
Cor got married in January, 1878. Their friendship continued to
grow, nevertheless, out of Loti's admiration for Le Cor's simplicity
and the sailor's respect for the writer's genius. On Loti's return from
Turkey, when he was stationed along the Brittany coast in 1878–1879,
he accompanied Le Cor on his visits to his native villages, admiring
the grimness of the rugged landscape and the beauty of the wild
flowers. In June, 1879, Loti in turn invited his friend home to Rochefort, where the strong sailor was able to carry Tante Lalie downstairs to
celebrate her ninetieth birthday with the family, and showed him
the garden of Limoise. In July, 1880, May and December, 1882,
and May, 1883, Loti stayed with Pierre and Marianne Le Cor and his
godson Lucien-Julien at their cottage in the small Breton village of

Rosporden; he attended with the Le Cors the Christmas mass in the old granite church at Rosporden in 1882 and also the *pardon* procession there in August, 1884, when, with his usual dandyism, he chose to wear the more elaborate, traditional Breton costume of the neighboring village of Elliant. Such was his enjoyment in their simple, honest company that he later confessed to Pouvillon that "my only friend in life, my comrade and brother, is a rather rascally sailor who can just about read"[6] and urged Mme Adam to use her influence to have Le Cor promoted to second *maître* in 1880 and *maître* in 1884. Loti's impressions of the Le Cors' existence are found in a letter to Plumkett of July, 1880:

Never before had I understood so well the poetic idyllicism of Brittany, the charm of the region's peace and antiquity. The old songs of Yves' mother as she rocks little Pierre, my godson, in his cradle handed down from another age; the pretty costumes of the young girls with their wide, pleated white collars and high *coiffes*.... And the paths full of honeysuckle and pink heather, the old, moss-coated oak trees, the peaceful countryside with its undefinable stillness of years gone by and small granite chapels dotted all over the woods ...

There is nothing more dangerous, more unhealthy, than this type of sensitive, sophisticated existence that we have made for ourselves, you and I. Get married quickly, try to be simple, to lead a quiet and honest family life, and believe in God....[7]

As was seen in *Fleurs d'Ennui*, Plumkett did take his friend's advice to get married; Loti was not so successful in his advances toward women or his pursuit of God, and resigned himself to merely admiring the vitality, virility and simple, pious Breton life of his sailor friend. However, like many sailors, Le Cor drank too much[8] and this vice constantly threatened the security of both his otherwise exemplary naval career and his tender love of his family. The sailor's fight against his weakness only made Loti appreciate all the more that primitive Breton simplicity and almost childish naïveté which made him so efficient at sea and so vulnerable once on land. It is this struggle that forms the framework of the plot of the novel, which, encouraged by Daudet, who had been impressed by his own sailor friend Madec's conquest of his alcoholism, Loti began to write after spending Christmas, 1882, with the Le Cors. The first part of it was completed in early 1883 while Loti was working in Rochefort, and sent to Pouvillon and Mme Lee Childe for their comments; in April the second section was finished, and by May Loti was arranging for its publication with a dedication to Daudet in the August-September issues of the *Revue des Deux Mondes;* however, the novel was not completed when Loti embarked on the "Atalante" bound for the Far East in June, and was only concluded a month later while he was sailing between Aden and Colombo.

Loti had referred to the novel in early 1883 in a letter to Pouvillon as "the work where I have included and I am still adding much from my own life,"[9] and *Mon Frère Yves* is to a large extent a literary transposition, with names and chronology slightly altered, of Loti's relations with Le Cor over the years. The ginger-haired, sun-tanned sailor with the athletic physique of a Greek statue and tattoos of fish and anchors on his chest and wrist[10] is introduced to the reader through the details of his *livret de marin*—a further example of Loti's fetishistic evocation of impressions by association with certain objects. A reference to the priest's refusal to ring the bells at Yves' christening at Saint Pol-de-Léon in August, 1851, because of his seafaring family's dissipation of their money on drink and the account of his temptation on landing at Brest twenty-four years later to celebrate with drink his gaining his first stripes, in spite of his awareness of the narrator's disapproval and his thoughts of his mother, indicate, however, the inherited weakness of this tall, quiet lad with a deep Breton accent and tender, childish smile, whose campaigns are recounted in the *livret*. Loti's description of Yves Kermadec at dawn the next morning as "a dark mass having human form lying in the gutter" and his punishment on board the "Magicien" —reduction of his shore leave and a day in the hold—anticipate the scenes later in the novel when he gets drunk with his comrades in a Siamese port and when he gets put in irons on the "Médée" at Brest—in reality on the "Tonnerre" at Cherbourg in May, 1878— after returning from the Far East.

But Loti's work is not simply an account of Yves succumbing to the family vice as in a Goncourt or Zola novel, nor is it a psychological study of Yves' struggle with his conscience; Loti stresses in some extremely touching scenes the sailor's sense of shame after the event, his aged mother's plea to the narrator to look after her son and keep him from temptation, as well as the narrator's efforts to rescue his friend from both drink and the authorities when in port;

but he is much more concerned to explain Yves' problem by the existence he leads as a Breton at sea. Loti's novel thus does not show its midshipman narrator criticizing his *gabier de hamac* on their various voyages together, but rather sympathizing with him and trying to keep him sober in his own best interests and in those of the young Breton girl Marie Keremen he marries and the son Pierre they soon have. It is not Yves but his Breton simplicity and primitive association with the sea that are to blame for his vulnerability to drink. Hence, the focussing of the scenes of Yves' life now on him at home in Plou-herzel (in reality Plounès-en-Goëtan), now on him on top of the yards at sea, and the various alternating insights given into the life led by sailors on board and by their wives at the ports in order to explain Yves' case within the general context of the Bretons and the sea.

Life in a Breton village and life at sea are equally simple and harsh; the alternating shots of Yves and the narrator's visits to the former's birthplace and native village and then of Yves on the yards during a storm off Cape Horn make this point clear by their juxta-position. The views Loti shows of Brittany—its bare, gorse-covered countryside with old granite churches and moss-coated towers; its friendly, honest people in regional costume who live in lonely, primitive cottages, speak with a Celtic accent and enjoy singing Breton airs; the sacrifice of their sons these close-knit communities are obliged to make to the lure of the sea; and the hard life of the women and children left behind queuing in the rain to receive their bread-winner's pay or standing, wrapped in drenched shawls and *coiffes,* on the jetty to witness the arrival or departure of their men-folk—emphasize the crude simplicity and unspoilt naturalness of the region. The close-up pictures he provides of the Kermadecs' life—the scenes, for example in Yves' friend Jean's cottage, where they eat *crêpes,* sing local songs, invoke the saints to protect them from the spirits outside in the howling wind, sleep alongside the animals they keep, and next morning collect seafood along the shore or *luze* fruits in the woods—and the more spectacular "tableaux of the spring procession at Saint Eloi de Toulven and the *pardon* at Plou-gastel, in which the Kermadecs participate serve to confirm this impression. For Loti, it is as if the Breton people with their native expressions and the "wretchedness and primitiveness of long ago" of their homes were, like the wild flowers and granite outcrops of the landscape, part of the unspoilt heritage of ancient Gaul; here, all is simple and natural, even the Breton's traditional love of church—seen at little Pierre's baptism with all its ceremony and superstition—and attachment to his family, shown in Yves' tender affection for his wife and son.

Yves epitomizes the Breton character in his primitive simplicity and appealing mixture of toughness and tenderness; he is therefore at home in the natural wilderness of the sea and makes a most careful and valiant sailor. Whether guiding the ship from his position on the mast during fog off the Brittany coast or in the still heat of the Coral Sea, helping the narrator with his hammock, washing down himself, his clothes or the ship's deck, or catching the passing gulls and flying fish, Yves is, with his pet owl beside him, always happily occupied at sea; for the sailor on a ship is as dependent on and involved with the vicissitudes of Nature as the Breton communities on the land; Loti's description of the storm at sea and the sufferings of the sailors on the yards makes this clear:

Sometimes the *Médée* reared up, rose above them as if she too were conspiring with the fury of the storm against them. But then she would subside again, prow foremost, into the treacherous troughs that followed the waves; she reached the very bottom of these sort of valleys which could be seen opening out between the high walls of water; and we longed to rise upward again and come out of these sloping, shiny green walls that seemed about to close in on us. . . .

Above, high on the masts, they were trying to tighten the topsails. . . . It was hard enough just holding on so as not to be pulled off, clinging to things that were all moving about, soaking wet and streaming with water; but now they had to also do their job up there, on yards that kept flapping about with sudden, jerky movements like some large, wounded bird in agony trying to beat its wings in a last effort.

Yves is virtually a child of the sea and the deep with its tempests, its calms, and its marine life "in as rudimentary a state as the dark waters of the prehistoric world were once in"; he lives in concert with Nature, often assuming an almost symbolic significance as he helps guide his ship in its mysterious destiny among the elements. Indeed, his whole being is so rudimentary and exposed like that of the sea he lives by and the land he comes from that he finds it difficult to settle down with his family and resist the pleasures of the ports after the months of fairly ascetic existence on board ship. As Marie remarks when he takes to drinking in Brest, he is "a big child whom sea life has ruined," a victim of the sea when on land, a prey to the corrupting influences of port and town. At first, his love of his young son rescues him from succumbing to his weakness, but eventually only the stern measures of the narrator save his friend from deserting the navy and his family from the misery described through the dialogue of the Breton women waiting for their husbands' return in the streets of Brest.

The novel thus has a somewhat idyllic ending with Yves, now sober, enjoying his new cottage at Toulven with his family[11] and receiving his stripes as *second maître* as he disembarks at Toulon in April, 1883. In fact, it might well be argued that Yves' development between his decision to leave home and desert from shame and his surprising reappearance on the "Primauguet" in the tropics, though technically an excellent use of the narrator's role to astonish the reader, is too rapid to explain his following henceforth the path of family happiness. However, if its psychological analysis is not as detailed as it might be, the novel's impressionistic descriptions of the sea's moods and the effects of light on it—be it the ripples made by sharks or the reflections of moonlight or sunset—are superb; Goncourt commented in fact that he would have preferred the novel without its biographical details.[12] The following passage on the sea at night may serve as an example: Loti uses the image of the lamps, the qualifying repetition of detail, and plurals to magnify the impressionistic effect of the mystery of the light in the vastness of the ocean:

> And the sea itself shone from below. There was a sort of immense, diffuse glow in the water. The slightest movements—the ship going slowly along, a shark turning about—created by their ripples splashes of luminous light. And so there flickered over the vast mirror-like surface of the sea thousands of such spontaneous flames of light, like small lamps that were suddenly and mysteriously lit everywhere, burned for a few moments, and then died away.

For *Mon Frère Yves* is not so much a portrait of Loti's sailor friend as a tribute to that primitive simplicity of Nature he inherited as a Breton and experienced in his contact with the oceans.

IV   Pêcheur d'Islande

Loti's attraction to the simple life close to Nature of the Breton people is reflected in what proved to be the most famous of his novels, *Pêcheur d'Islande,* which won him the Prix Vitet, went into over two hundred editions by 1900, and connected his name forever with Brittany, as the Quai Pierre Loti at Paimpol testifies. It was begun at Rochefort as a short story entitled "Au Large" in early 1885, almost a year after his return from his first trip to Indo-China, and, at Alphonse Daudet's and Mme Adam's suggestion, was enlarged and mostly completed during Loti's stay in the Far East in late 1885 and published from March to June, 1886, in the *Nouvelle Revue* of Mme Adam,[13] to whom it was dedicated. Loti had seen quite a lot of Breton life during his stays at Brest or Lorient prior to or after his various voyages, and his close friendship with the Le Cors had endeared Brittany to him. Its appeal had been all the greater in December, 1882, when he was attracted to a young girl from a family of Iceland fishermen he met at Guingamp; unfortunately, she was already engaged to one of the fishermen, and Loti's dreams of recapturing the simplicity of his early life through marriage were banished.[14] However, Loti saw her again in October, 1884, and tried once more to entice her by proposing to meet her at Saint Brieuc; but by December she canceled the date and Loti in despair rushed to Guingamp to urge her to change her mind; she was adamant, however, and the most Loti received was a parting kiss. This second rebuff only made Loti's desire to be integrated in a simple life all the more frustrating and the difference between his world and that of the fisherfolk all the more evident to him. Obsessed with this vain desire and documented by his stays with the Le Cors when he attended the annual *pardon* procession and his visits while at Guingamp and Paimpol to the fisherfolk's chapel at Pors Even and to some of the local people's homes,[15] he began writing his story: that of a fisherman's allegiance being divided between the sea he lives with and the girl he loves, between the primitive world of Nature and the civilized world of Man, and his loved-one's tragic sacrifice of him to the sea which finally claims him.

Originally, the story was basically that of Loti's own experience of the Breton girl's persistence in waiting for her loved-one's return; but he later cut out certain scenes where this was too obvious for the sake of the girl, and changed his title just as he also had some of the lovemaking episodes curtailed because it was out of keeping with the impression of Breton life he wished to convey. He had thought at one point of asking the Navy to send him to Iceland so that he could "make a more beautiful book,"[16] but when he was ordered back to the Orient instead, he decided to leave Iceland in the background of the novel and concentrate more on the sea and Breton life. Thus, he based part of the storm scene on a storm he watched while in Indo-China and evoked in his mind the Breton landscape amid the sun and heat of the Far East by thinking of the girl who had refused him. This must have been quite a *tour de force* when it is considered that he completed the novel while living in Nagasaki and, later, touring Japan, and proves perhaps the deep sense of nostalgia with which both Brittany and his desired romance there had left him.

As in *Mon Frère Yves,* Loti alternates his shots of life at sea and the existence of those remaining behind on the land in order not only to provide an overall picture of the lives of the Breton fisherfolk, but to stress in particular the underlying similarity of the two modes of living. First, Loti shows the six men on board the "Marie" out fishing off the coast of Iceland where they spend the whole of the spring and summer months. It is 11 P.M. and, dressed in blue jerseys and oilskin caps or *suroît,* smoking at their pipes, these *Islandais* huddle round the table under the swaying lamp and chat of their past experiences and their homes before turning in to their small bunks or taking the night shift on deck. The atmosphere is damp with the steam of their drying clothes, space is extremely limited, and their furniture is rough and well worn, but these tall, muscular fishermen who have to bend in half like bears in order to move about inside the boat are at home in this "giant empty sea-gull": for, as is seen shortly afterward when they begin hauling in the catch, these men are like "large sea birds" with a primitive, almost savage understanding of and devotion to Nature, a childish timidity in social matters on the land, a chaste reserve with regard to women, and a simple, traditional faith in the powers of the Virgin whose effigy dominates their cabin.

Yann is typical of them. His late arrival on the scene in the cabin, his huge, virile body bent in two in order to descend through the small entrance hole in the ceiling and with a "wild, proud expres-

sion" on his face, makes his figure all the more imposing.[17] Like
his young friend Sylvestre, Yann's outer toughness hides a vir-
ginally chaste, childishly naïve personality with the same diaphanous, pure, and primitive qualities as the calm sea at dawn,
which still retains all the sanctity of the very first Creation. He
enjoys the pleasures of the ports, recognizing them for the little
they are worth, but takes pride above all in his partnership with the
sea; this is seen in the storm episode, when the sea erupts into
gigantic waves tossing the "Marie" about like a toy amid the
Apocalyptic confusion of wind and darkness and Yann and
Sylvestre stay at the wheel trying to guide the craft, singing Breton
airs and crossing themselves as they do so, like "two hardy creatures instinctively clinging on so as not to die"; despite the slabs
of water drenching them and the whirling of the elements around
them, they defy the blind forces of inexorable Nature with an
animal tenacity as wild and primitive as the oceans themselves; and
just as Yann struggles against the stormy outburst of the sea that
suddenly shatters the calm of earlier, so he defies the welling passion
of Gaud, the young and beautiful girl he met at the Paimpol *pardon*
before his departure for Icelandic waters, and his own growing
affection for her.

Gaud belongs, like Yann, to the traditional yet primitive world of
Brittany; she is serious and proud like her family and ancestors,
all of whom were Iceland fishermen; she wears the *coiffe*
headdress of all Breton women and has the same air of purity about
her as her grandmother, Mme Moan, with whom she lives; she has
lovely blond hair, which adds a pagan touch to her pious air and
makes her resemble a "druidess of the forest" in the bare, primitive
Breton countryside. Even a brief stay in Paris with her father has not
completely destroyed the simple Breton in her; it has made her more
sophisticated in her manner and dress than her friends, but also made
her appreciate more on her return the antiquity and simplicity of
Brittany and the related mixture of wildness and childishness in
Yann at their second meeting at a wedding. But despite the traditional
Breton setting of their two meetings at the *pardon* and the wedding—
symbolizing the mournful and joyful aspects that make up Breton life
and anticipating the novel's tragic close—and her artful connivance
in trying to see Yann on his return from Iceland, she does not manage
to encourage him to contemplate marrying her; indeed, her visit
to the ancient, wind-swept Pors Even chapel with its moss-covered

granite walls, well-worn wooden benches, countless memorials to fishermen lost at sea, and ancient effigy of the Virgin resembling pagan Cybele and "recalling the wildness of an earlier age," convinces her of the Breton fisherfolk's and, in particular, Yann's family's primitive dedication to the sea. Yann's silence and his subsequent refusal of her because she is so much wealthier and more refined than he merely confirm her suspicions of his devotion to the sea and make her love all the more desperate as he leaves again for Iceland; finally, his resistance to her and sacrifice of his love are symbolized, as in the storm earlier, by the "Marie's" temporary foundering on rocks off the Icelandic coast and its refloating itself soon after.

The value of Yann's sacrifice of his love is stressed by Sylvestre's similarly valiant sacrifice of himself in Indo-China; the Breton spirit is used to acts of bravery and self-sacrifice, having been nurtured by years of struggling with the elements and losing its sons at sea; and those fisherfolk left behind are used to the suffering such losses cause. Loti's account of Sylvestre's departure for the Far East, of his bravery on the field of battle, of his death in a ship's stifling sick bay, his anonymous grave in a Singapore cemetery, and of his aged grandmother Mme Moan's shock at hearing of his death—much of it based on Loti's own experiences of recovering from sunstroke in the ship's sick bay and witnessing a sailor's funeral at Singapore on his voyage to Indo-China, and much of it reminiscent of Gustave Viaud's death at sea—provide some of the most tender scenes he ever wrote and a rare tribute to the Christian suffering of these simple but hardy people. Now Mme Moan and Gaud support each other in their hardship and distress; the old woman has lost virtually the last of her vast family; the young girl is penniless after her father's death and languishes away waiting for her loved-one; only the wind howling outside their bare, cold cottage accompanies their own plaintive sighs. Even Yann's brief return brings Gaud no solace for he ignores her and she continues living an empty, gloomy existence looking after the increasingly senile Mme Moan. It is, however, a common feeling of protection and pity for the old lady, whose cat has been killed by some local children, that brings Yann and Gaud together, and it is the two women's reduced circumstances that now encourages Yann to seek her hand.

If the red color of the sea and the flocks of birds dying on the

deck of his ship anticipate symbolically Sylvestre's death on his
voyage to Tourane, Yann's enrollment on a new boat, the "Léopoldine," after so many trips on the "Marie" and the circumstances of
his wedding seem to announce for him a similar tragic *dénouement*.
As soon as she overhears that Yann has enlisted on the "Léopoldine," Gaud is filled with an intuitive anxiety. When on their
wedding day the spring weather suddenly becomes tempestuous,
the wind so whips up the sea that they must abandon the traditional
visit to the *islandais* chapel of the Trinity on the cliff face, and
the couple have to battle their way back to Mme Moan's cottage
through the gales to celebrate their wedding night together, it is
clear, as Yann observes, that "the sea is not pleased because I
promised to marry her" and Nature is having its revenge. The
wedded couple, like the fisherfolk singing at the party, might forget
the sea and wind outside in their lovemaking, but the prayers for
the departed before the celebrations and their awareness of the
Islandais' imminent departure make Gaud realize that her hold
over Yann is but temporary and he is "migratory like some great
sea bird"; she therefore resigns herself to accepting his leaving
for the land of the midnight sun, of fjords and treeless landscapes,
as part of their new destiny. Their fate is, however, a tragic one,
for, as Loti states with brutal brevity: "He never returned." The
"Léopoldine" like the "Reine Berthe," which the crew of the
"Marie" meet in the fog, vanishes mysteriously without trace and
Gaud is left ignorant of her husband's fate, praying for his safe
return in the Pors Even chapel and gazing out over the calm but
indifferent sea with its autumnal mantle of gray mist. The crucifixes along the shore have little influence now on Yann's destiny,
for it is Nature and the sea which finally reclaim him from Gaud's
delicate hold and possess him in their wild and mortal embrace.

As in *Mon Frère Yves,* it is the sea that dominates the novel;
it epitomizes the primeval simplicity and unspoilt naturalness
Loti sought in an increasingly civilized world; and it kept alive in
those who lived with it and understood its moods a primitive wild
spontaneity of feeling and action and nurtured a sort of pagan
devotion in them—qualities that had virtually disappeared from the
oversophisticated skeptical society of France. If *Mon Frère Yves*
reveals the simple, traditional life of the Breton people, *Pêcheur
d'Islande* relates their existence more explicitly to the sea and the

role and fate of those who live by it. The sea in the former novel was the changing background for Yves' unsettled life, while in the latter work it represents Man's contact with Nature and the chaotic forces of early evolution, as, for example, in the storm scene:

> A gigantic medley of noises came from everywhere like a prelude to the Apocalypse evoking the terror of the end of the world. Thousands of voices could be heard in it: from above, booming or whining ones, which seemed almost far away on account of their vastness: These were of the wind, the great spirit behind this cataclysm, the invisible force controlling it all. It was frightening; but there were other sounds nearer, more substantial and threatening in their urge to destroy, which came from the sea, seething and crackling in its turmoil as if on fire. . . .

While in the storm episode of *Mon Frère Yves* Loti is more at pains to describe the severity of a sailor's life on board ship, here he is depicting the sea as an untamed creation of Nature, mysterious and wild, the fatal factor controlling the lives and values of the Breton fisherfolk. And it is for this reason—because the *pêcheurs d'Islande* were in such intimate contact with the primeval and natural—that he so admired their traditional simplicity and faith.

V *Developments in Loti's Approach*

Loti's approach in the "Breton" novels just analyzed is basically the same as that found in his early "exotic" works; for Brittany was for Loti just as exotically different and distant as the lands overseas he had described and was therefore treated with the same discriminating impressionistic detachment. His stress on the primitive, primeval, and animal in these novels through the imagery of his descriptions and his choice of incidents show that his total impressions of Brittany and the Bretons were just as exaggerated and poetically romanticized as those of his "exotic" works. If *Pêcheur d'Islande* is impressive on account of its style, it is because he has perfected here what was still an immature technique in *Le Mariage de Loti* or *Le Roman d'un Spahi*. The point of view and stylistics of his type of impressionism remain the same; the same roving viewpoint is found in the texture of the narrative—for example, in the scene of Sylvestre's farewell to his grandmother (Part II, Chapter 8)—with its mixture of reported speech, indirect free speech, plain narrative interior monologue, dialogue, impersonal constructions, and retrospective comments from the author and also in the structure of the novels where Loti focusses now on one setting and now on another with a similar cinematographic dexterity; and the characters are still functional and their outlook and feelings reflected in and explained by their setting, as in Gaud's visit to the fishermen's chapel while awaiting Yann's return (Part V, Chapter 7). Here, however, Loti spends longer on each of his shots, the action is more self-contained, and plot and moral theme are more prominent; the novel is being used to convey a positive message on a more accessible aspect of French life without making any comparison of the exotic and Europe. For, as the critic René Doumic[18] observed, *Mon Frère Yves* and *Pêcheur d'Islande* strike a new note in Loti's output by their lack of cynicism, and it is clear that in them Loti was expressing his own moral and spiritual desire to escape from the cultural and literary hothouse of contemporary society that nurtured his *Fleurs d'Ennui* and integrate himself in the simple life close to Nature and God of Brittany. Unfortunately, Pierre Loti could not revert to the simple outlook and belief of Julien Viaud as he desired, for, as Henry Bordeaux commented,[19] his stress on the values of the primitive was but a reflection of his "decadent" outlook of sophisticated nostalgia.

CHAPTER 4

An Exile in Asia

I *Indo-China*

IF *Mon Frère Yves* and *Pêcheur d'Islande* reflect Loti's desire
to return to the simplicity and naturalness of his childhood, which
he associated with the life of the Bretons, and to depart from the
literary sophistication of *Fleurs d'Ennui* and his earlier romances,
his visits to the Far East at this time served to aggravate his sense
of physical isolation from France and spiritual exile from Brittany
and accentuate his desire to regain his innocence and former self.
Loti embarked on the "Atalante" for Indo-China in late May,
1883, when Annam, one of the provinces of French Indo-China,
transferred its allegiance to China and the French government
under Jules Ferry decided to teach the mandarins a lesson. His
journey there was not uneventful, for the ship passed over the spot
in the Bay of Bengal where Loti's brother had been buried at
sea, and Loti himself suffered from sunstroke and was nursed by
his sailor friend Le Scoarnec. Furthermore, once they reached
Singapore in late July, 1883, they were in the "yellow hell" of
Southeast Asia with the "simian bustle" of its Chinese population,
its grotesque temple guardians, its damp heat and fever-infested
swamps; gone were the handsome men and women of India and
the scorching desert of Egypt; Indo-China with its strange people,
Oriental culture, and unhealthy climate is for Loti "a real land of
exile where nothing attracts or charms me" when he lands in
Halong Bay and proceeds upriver to Tourane; moreover, there
was a war on in this inhospitable land.

Loti published an account of the French campaign there in
three articles (the first two anonymously) in *Le Figaro* on 28
September and 13 and 17 October 1883, describing the French
bombardment of the forts of Tuan-An near Hué between 18 and
20 August, which he witnessed. His description of the French
ships' shelling of the Annamites' forts on the first two days and
the landing of the sailors on the next, followed by the capture of

the Northern and Southern circular forts and the burning and
pillaging of nearby villages, caused an uproar in France.[1] In
particular, the gruesome depiction of a sailor bayoneting an
Annamite through the mouth and neck and of corpses with eyes
gouged out and skulls battered; ironic exclamations on the
magnificent flames that the Eden-like villages nearby produced
as they burned and on the success of the sailors' frivolous pillaging
as reminiscent of the invasions of Attila and Genghis Khan;
references to the bravery and primitiveness of the natives—"they
did not have the look of a real enemy; they were all killed where
they stood, petrified with fear, by repeated bayoneting"; and
remarks on the sailors' panic and hysteria such as "they carried on
killing almost with relish, so exhilarated were they by all the
shouting, running about and blood everywhere" brought strong
reaction from the Navy and government; for such comments
revealed only too clearly the opposition which Loti like so many
of his countrymen felt for the whole colonial venture in Annam.

In actual fact, Loti felt sorry for both sides in the war: He
pitied the innocent, brave Bretons, whom he saw playing on their
biniou pipes or sitting in silent apprehension on the eve of battle,
being forced to fight against the cunning and wicked Chinese
Huns under King Tu-Duc; and he also felt pity for the panic-stricken
Annamites who were defenseless against the French forces and
fled either into the river or into the villages where they burned
to death in the flames engulfing their huts and temples. Even after
the peace treaty is signed, Loti's sympathy is clearly divided
between the French sailors, whose innocence the government has
exploited and who are merely glad to be leaving without having
lost a man and with plenty of souvenirs pillaged from the ruins of
villages, and the Annamites, who still try to retain their self-respect
and strange culture despite their crushing defeat by the West
just as King Tu-Duc remains unharmed and unseen in his
mysterious citadel.

The French government did not, however, share Loti's views
and, despite his protests to Daudet and Mme Adam about the
veracity of his account and his sympathy for his sailor friends,[2]
he is recalled to France on 28 November; he sails for Toulon on
the "Corrèze" on 16 December 1883 and is put at first on half-pay
and then on the supernumerary list for the next year. Between

the capture of the forts and his recall, Loti has, however, a chance
to see more of Annam and records his impressions of this and his
voyage home in *Propos d'Exil,* published in 1884–85 in the *Revue
des Deux Mondes* and dedicated to Mme Lee-Childe, Loti's
hostess in Paris, who had recently died.

II   Propos d'Exil

Two episodes during Loti's short stay in Indo-China demon-
strate his feeling of being exiled from France and European culture: his journey on 24 August to Tourane to receive the surrender
of one of the mandarins after the war and his visit on 1 December
to the subterranean temples of Marble Mountain. In the first of
these, Loti remarks particularly on the ugliness of the people,
the wretchedness of their huts, and the macabre quality of the
grimacing china animals guarding the Buddhist temples. Nature
alone—the musk aroma of the lush jungle and the beauty of the
wild orchids—compensates a little for the strangeness of the place,
epitomized for Loti in the hideous temple figures that shatter any
affinity the rest of the rustic landscape may have in his mind with
provincial France; for, as his visit to Marble Mountain shows, they
belong to a religion and culture that has its primitive roots in a
totally different understanding of the universe from the European
conception of God. On this visit, Loti climbs up steps carved into
the mountain slopes amid the spiral tombs of the mandarins until
he reaches the top and can look down into several pagodas sunk
into the mountain and containing rows of gold-plated grotesque
idols; he then descends a path of marble steps bordered with
periwinkle and other tropical plants that leads into an avenue of
grotesque idols, some draped with the hoods of monks, others
bare and worm-eaten, and on through a great door—"the gateway
to the Beyond"—into a deep, dark cavern hung with lianas from
which snakes, bats, and orangutans suspend themselves; the
grimaces of the rows of idols set back in the marble walls, the stares
of the orangutans, the sinister Buddhic silence of the whole place,
the underwater coloring of this subterranean pagoda with its hidden
altars and phantomlike priests—"it was like going inside an enormous emerald pierced by a ray of moonlight"—make this an exciting but frightening experience for Loti. The weirdness of all these

idols with their multiple arms, lascivious gestures, glaring fat faces, and grimacing expressions and the primitive antiquity of their worship in the Marble Mountain convince Loti of the remoteness of the Oriental world from the European since the earliest times.

The rest of *Propos d'Exil* is largely an account of Loti's voyage to France and his return a year later, and his short stops at Singapore, Mahé in India, and Obock in Somaliland. Loti's very remoteness from France makes him nostalgic of home, but the slightest association with his childhood or element of French life overseas such as the colonial influence on Mahé or the Breton sailors in Annam cause him to realize the gulf that divides the two civilizations of Asia and Europe and that separates the exotic Pierre Loti from Julien Viaud's neo-Breton existence in Rochefort. He was made conscious of his straddling two worlds and two sorts of existence by the misinterpretation of his articles on the Annam war in France and his recall home. In *Sur la Mort de l'Admiral Courbet,* his tribute to the commander of the French fleet in Annam, who died in June, 1885, Loti implies that the theater of war in Annam is too far away from France for people there to appreciate the great loss his death represents and that only the sailors who served under him can realize it.

This outer remoteness which Loti had actually felt in Asia reflected also that inner one he felt between his two selves; the contrast, in the short tale *Un Vieux,* between the retired Breton sailor Kervella's memories of his youth and voyages overseas and his exotic souvenirs and static, senile existence now in his cottage on the Brest-Portzic road is in fact a pessimistic, morbid transposition of Loti's view of himself on his return to France in early February, 1884. He keeps his mother and aunt company, visits Oleron, Limoise and Brittany, and tries to court a Breton girl, but the world of youthful simplicity and his childhood is closed to him and he can but long for it and the unsophisticated life among sailors, of which he is presently deprived, in his novels on Breton life. On the other hand, he is bored by his situation and frustrated by his sense of failure and by the monotony of Rochefort, especially when his niece Ninette marries, and needs the company of Parisian celebrities and his exotic souvenirs of overseas to overcome them. Dismissal from the navy would have deprived him of both the simplicity and vitality of life at sea and his escapist, sophisticated taste for overseas, and he openly confessed he could not live without the naval life he was used to.[3] Fortunately, thanks to Mme Adam's maternal defense of his cause with the naval authorities, Loti receives an order on 3 March 1885 to return to the Far East. On 20 March he thus embarks on the "Mytho" at Toulon bound for Ma-Kung, where he transfers on 5 May to the "Triomphante," which in early July takes him and his friend Le Cor, who is also on board, to Japan.

III   Madame Chrysanthème

From the very beginning when Loti first heard he was bound for Japan, he does not seem to have been particularly excited at the prospect; perhaps the Chinese race did not appeal to him after his experiences in Annam or his horizons were too clouded by his gloom of the past year; whatever the reason, he told his niece on 2 July 1885: "I'm quite happy at the prospect of going on tomorrow to Japan, but no more than I should be."[4] His immediate plans were to rent a little house with paper shutters in a suburb of Nagasaki and to relax there and complete *Pêcheur d'Islande* while the "Triomphante" was in dry dock for repairs. However, encouraged by Yves and "having nothing to do and feeling lonely,"[5] he "marries" on a temporary basis a Japanese girl, Okané-San, soon after his arrival and they live together in the house of an elderly lady, Kaka-San, from 8 July to 12 August. Okané is "pleasant and a little sad," plays the samisen well, and can prepare tea in traditional style, but by early August Loti is bored both by her and her country. He writes to Ninette on 7 August: "I still feel bored but am doing all I can to get interested in this country. It's impossible, though—it baffles me too much!"[6] He described his relations with his Japanese wife and her country in his novel *Madame Chrysanthème,* dedicated to the Duchesse de Richelieu and published in December, 1887.

As in Annam, Loti's first impressions of Japan are of the people's ugliness; his fantastic ideas about Japan, encouraged by the awesome cliff corridor entrance to Nagasaki through which his ship sails into port, are shattered when the deck is invaded by hordes of little smiling and bowing traders carrying a vast variety of goods. "How ugly, shabby, and grotesque all these people were!" he remarks. The fact that it is pouring with rain as he arrives does not improve his impression and it is only the magical reflections of the mountains' shadows and the shoreline's lanterns in the water that resemble the Japan he had imagined. His trip in the "floating coffin" of a sampan propelled by children to the shore and his ride through a wet, muddy Nagasaki, driven by one of the rickshawmen in straw rainwear, "a species of human hedgehog," to the *Jardin des Fleurs* teahouse, where he is greeted by two girls, "in postures of complete submission," simply add to his astonished amusement. It is only when he is seated like a Buddha on a velvet cushion in the center of the empty teahouse, after his shoes and umbrella have been carefully removed and a snack set before him with a series of gentle smiles and bows from his two hostesses, that Loti is able to take stock of his surroundings while awaiting the arrival of Mr. Kangeroo-San who will find him a Japanese wife. He finds the room itself rather glacial in its neat bareness, but he is amused by the politeness of his two hostesses. Dressed in silken kimonos, they remind him, with their powdered faces, slit eyes, rouged cheeks, and red lips and tiny, delicate movements, of little dolls; and when he goes with Yves and an excessively polite Mr. Kangeroo-San, dressed in bowler hat and white gloves, to choose a wife from amongst a small selection of girls brought along by their mothers for the purpose and discovers Chrysanthemum, he feels amid all the ladies' mechanical curtsies and bows that he has got married "among marionettes." Indeed, after he is married at the police station and has paid the required amount for the "hire" of his "wife," he refers to her as a fairy, sees his home with its stork-patterned paper screens, small tables with odd vases of flowers, and gilt statue of Buddha as "a doll's house," and looks down at the twinkling lights of Nagasaki below their apartment at Diou-djen-dji as a "fairy-tale setting."

If Loti is amused by the smallness and delicacy of his "Nippon doll" and the conventional and artificial politeness of Japanese people, already anticipated as he entered port by his view of the artificially arranged landscape around a pagoda, he is frustrated and bored by the lack of real communication between himself and Chrysanthemum. He watches her light her candles to Buddha, prepare her meals of rice, bamboo, seaweed, chopped sparrow and stuffed prawn, lie down on the floor at night on her cushion and wooden pillow, and smoke her pipe before sleeping, but he cannot enjoy her company; for not only is she quiet and reflective—an indication, like her symbolic name, of her aristocratic origins and her representative role as an incarnation of Imperial Japan in the novel—but her world is like that of the Annamites, so remote and inaccessible to Loti.

When they go out together with Yves and some of their neighbors, including their proprietress Madame Prune, to the teahouse or the Osueva temple, Loti is enchanted by their lantern procession and finds the shops where they buy fans, toys, or cakes and the pilgrimage they witness quite curious, but he cannot understand the Japanese way of life or mentality; he cannot understand why the Japanese, normally so conscious of etiquette, treat death so lightly and gaily when he watches a funeral; he is a little shocked at the openness with which such an affected people bathe in the nude; he is delighted at the Japanese love of their children, but is surprised at the mixture of the childish and the macabre in their toys and kites; he cannot distinguish gaiety from fear in the pilgrims' masked procession and is as astonished by the colossal size and gruesome statues of the temple as by the comfortable life led by its effeminate priests; in short, the strange mixture in Japanese culture of the ugly and the delicate, the gruesome and the pretty, the simple and the affected, the natural and the artificial, which Loti sees epitomized in the group of women posing at the photographer's where he and Chrysanthemum are waiting to have their portraits taken, remains an enigma to him and often prompts a "smile of slight mockery" as he views the world around him with mystified detachment.

Instead, therefore, of evoking sensations of love and anguished desire for its continuance, Loti's relations with Chrysanthemum give rise to nostalgic regrets of past romances and evoke all the disillusionment of his lost youth and childhood; he compares his situation in Nagasaki with that in Istanbul, contrasting Chrysanthemum's reaction to the discovery of mice in their room to that of Aziyadé and his being awakened once by his neighbor the muezzin and now by Madame Prune's clapping below to summon the Shinto gods; the sound of the typhoon winds like the Japanese climate in general reminds him of home, but whereas the gales in the forests of Limoise seemed to carry forth the ideals and dreams of his childhood, those in the cryptomeria avenues here just give vent to his sense of boredom and frustration. It is not surprising, then, that he throws away through his porthole as he leaves Nagasaki the lotus blossoms Chrysanthemum has given him as a farewell token; he has not been able to establish real contact with her any more than with the country she represents; she hides under her conventional "marionette-like trappings" just as Japan does beneath a traditional culture that is "miniature, affected, and finical"; it seems to Loti, as he watches the craftsmen of Nagasaki applying an excess of attention and skill to the traditional pattern on not a few but hundreds of vases, as if the whole country has become mummified in an obsolescent cultural sophistication that has lost all contact with the present reality it is now grafted onto and is approaching its end in static, decadent affectation. Japan is "doll-size, antiquated, and drained of its vigor and vitality," strange and inaccessible, arousing but not satisfying the curiosity of the European, who, as in Loti's relationship with the symbolic Chrysanthemum, can only smile or admire but not understand; it appeals to his aesthetic dilettantism and spiritual detachment as an inanimate exotic object and his frustrating, passing fascination with it reflects the decadent, impersonal sophistication of his taste for the exotic and his consequent nostalgia for the simplicity and vitality of the past, which it has virtually suppressed.

IV   Japoneries d'Automne

On 12 August 1885, Loti's ship, the "Triomphante," left Nagasaki for Chéfou in Indo-China, where some of the sick and wounded including his friend Le Cor were sent back to France, and then returned to Japan, stopping at Kobe from 23 September to 8 October and at Yokohama from 11 October to 17 November before sailing via Hong Kong and Saigon to Europe. Deprived of Le Cor's company and determined not to engage in any new Japanese "marriage" after his experiences with Okané-San, Loti used this second stay to explore the country. In early October he goes from Kobe to the former Shogunate capital of Kioto and writes to his niece after visiting the temples and palaces there that he is "amazed by this old Japan which I had not expected to find";[7] in the first week of November he visits the sacred mountain of Nikko

with its magnificent shrines and reports home: "Such splendor
in such a mysterious forest setting makes these shrines something
quite unique";[8] and on 10 November he is invited to the traditional
chrysanthemum festival at the Imperial Palace at Edo, where the
Empress made one of her two annual appearances in public, and
comments to Ninette: "It's impossible to convey the charm of
such a person."[9] In short, Loti discovered traditional, old Japan
on his second stay there and gained insight into the original
Japanese culture which lay moribund beneath the contemporary
veneer of decadent oversophistication and was threatened by the
concomitant Westernization that accompanied its decline. The
fact that he was aware of witnessing the end of the old aristocratic
Japan of exquisite artistry, the final glimmer of its former power
and brilliance, and that he was seeing it in autumn at chrysanthemum time prompted him to give the title *Japoneries d'Automne*
to the volume, formed from articles on his visit published in the
Nouvelle Revue, Grande Revue, and *Revue des Deux Mondes*
in 1888.

Loti receives this impression of Japan's cultural twilight and the
passing of its earlier civilization and traditions particularly on his
visits to Kioto, Kamakura, and Nikko and during his attendance
at the Imperial chrysanthemum festival. Kioto, with its three
thousand temples and shrines, its Shogunate castle, and myriad
of alleyways and low, wooden houses, is but a relic of earlier
Japanese cultural glory; although Loti marvels at the "striking
anatomical realism" and "refined, skillfully evoked hideousness"
of the devilish cadaverous monsters with grimacing faces and
dozens of arms he finds in the old Buddhist temples of this "vast
lumber-room of religion" and is impressed by the primitive
simplicity of Shintoism with its bare shrines in the cryptomeria
forests and *tori* gateways, Kioto has for him the air of a "ghost
town" as he looks down on it enshrouded in autumn mist from the
Yasaka tower. It is above all when he visits the Nijo Castle palace
and marvels at the "bygone splendor" of its golden walls and
ceilings and sculptured friezes of flowers and birds and the silence
of its dim rooms, empty but for their bamboo mats and blinds,
that he becomes aware of the air of "very gradual effacement"
which the passing of time has lent to the former brilliance of Kioto's
past; the palace is now so silent and calm and yet still so exquisite

despite its faded colors that he feels as if he is in the residence of some "Sleeping Beauty" of long ago; even the dwarf shrubs and trees of the indoor miniature gardens seem to have lost their unreal dimensions in the passage of time and to appear more weathered and taller.

Unfortunately, it is impossible for a European to try to evoke in his mind the former splendor of Japan for "the differences in our origins create a great chasm between old Japan and us"; Loti can no more imagine the palace in Kioto inhabited by warrior princes and courtiers than he can fully evoke the fierce, chivalrous spirit of the forty-seven Samurai, who sacrificed themselves for the honor of their prince in 1630 and whose tombs he visits. Thus, when he goes to Kamakura and discovers that the giant Buddha, which now stands isolated in the middle of a forest like "some primitive colossal statue of a sleepy, melancholy monkey," and the diaphanous, beautifully patterned robes of the Empress Gzinégou-Koyo of 200 A.D. are all that remain of this former capital's glory, he is filled with melancholy at the thought of this lost past; the autumnal setting and the imminent sunset merely add to his sadness as the temple priests fold up again the Empress's robes and he looks out upon the forest and gardens where once there were palaces and warriors.

It is the nostalgia for the past generated by this feeling of autumnal melancholy that Loti savors on his visit to the magnificent temples and shrines of Nikko; here, Loti really feels as he is guided through the dark cryptomeria forests and over the sacred bridge to this mountainous Mecca of old Japan that he is entering into contact with the past. All is silent and dark around him; he is startled and awestruck by the "imposing grandeur" and "green twilight" of the giant trees; he is aware of following a path taken by Emperors, warriors, and pilgrims through the ages; and as he passes through isolated hamlets and by wayside shrines that have remained unchanged for centuries, he feels in communion with the past and the forest around him just as the mystics and artists of Nikko once did. His entry into Japan's past glory is symbolized in his description of the autumn sunset's effects on the forest leading to the sacred mountain and is evoked in terms of an almost religious emotion suggestive of his desire for the faith of Nikko:

Soon it became something quite magical. In the direction of the sunset the wood, now yellow and almost bare of leaves, is so impregnated and penetrated with golden light that, seen from the corridor of shadow where we are, it seems to be on fire. And these enormous trees along our path, these great, smooth pillars already of a reddish tone, bear the reflections of a fierce blaze. On the ground, the elongated shadows alternate with shafts of light and create patterns of black and golden rays, which continue in front of us virtually indefinitely. And away up in the vault of the forest there are great shafts of light which enter like those penetrating the darkness of a church in the evening. It was like some fiery apotheosis in a primitive temple. . . .

Unlike in Kioto and Kamakura, the gold-covered gateways and shrines of Nikko with their magnificent gargoyles and friezes of animals, dragons and birds, which Loti describes in great detail, have not been completely abandoned as empty relics of a distant past; in fact, the dances and worship here of the priests and priestesses of Shinto keep the past alive to some extent; Loti thus feels he has penetrated a little way into the traditional heart of old Japan as he watches and listens to the dance of the priestesses in scarlet and white and the rites of the priests in their flowing robes and hoods. Loti gains another final glimpse of old Japan when he attends the Imperial Palace in Edo for the chrysanthemum festival; the glistening, traditional robes of the Imperial ladies-in-waiting and the rare and exquisite delicacy of the Empress with her "air of a marble goddess" are as lovely and as refined as the rows of large pink chrysanthemums the small party of select visitors look down upon in the palace gardens. But just as the flowers will fade, so too will old Japan; this is implied in Loti's description of the Empress and her entourage returning to the palace like "large, fantastic moths of the twilight" silhouetted against the red of the November sunset.

The original culture of old Japan has now evolved into a decadent cult of shallow affectation and imitation, as was seen in *Madame Chrysanthème,* and is gradually being undermined and transformed by Western practices. This erosion of the old Japanese way of life is indicated not only by changes in dress—the frock coats worn by the town councillors of Utsunomya, the bowler hats of workers on an Edo tram, the evening gowns of the women at the ball at Roku-Meikau—but is also visible in the introduction of European music at the ball and at the Imperial Palace, of Western architecture and transport in the towns, and of foreign visitors into the country and at the Imperial court; in fact, when Loti attends the ball everything is so Europeanized that only the Japanese flags and faces remind him where he is. Loti is at once struck by the Japanese ability to imitate and amused by the ridiculous results of their efforts both at the ball and on the tram he takes to Asukusa. Clearly, there was little hope of the original Japan of Kioto and Nikko, of the Shoguns and the Samurai, of Oriental craftsmanship and Shinto simplicity, surviving the country's cultural decadence and slow Westernization. Hence, Loti is trying to capture in *Japoneries d'Automne* with his usual realistic impressionism "this last glimmer of a civilization about to die." And so, apart from the odd humorous incident, the mood of the volume is one of sentimental curiosity and nostalgic melancholy: curiosity about the old Japan he has just discovered and melancholy at the thought of its imminent passing forever.

On 10 February 1886, Loti arrived back in France after ten months away in the Far East and is posted to the "Magicien" at Rochefort for four months. In his works on Japan, Loti shows that that country's original simplicity and traditional vigor had been suppressed, like the innocence and idealism of his own childhood, by the contemporary decadent sophistication of an ancient culture now in process of rapid decline and transformation;[10] its imminent passing indicated Loti's own progress further and further away from the days of Limoise and his origins in Rochefort and Oleron. Thus, if his first voyage to Indo-China, described in *Propos d'Exil,* stressed his geographical remoteness from France, his visit to Japan and his comments on its affectation and decadence and nostalgia for its past splendor made him desire all the more to revert to the values of his lost childhood; it is then not without significance that *Pêcheur d'Islande* was completed during Loti's second stay in the Orient. The fact that it was followed by *Madame Chrysanthème* with its exotic interest in Japanese sophistication merely reveals the contradictory personality that tried to be both Julien Viaud and Pierre Loti.

CHAPTER 5

A Pilgrimage into the Past

I *Loti's Marriage*

FOR years Loti had looked to marriage as a solution to his desire to regain the simplicity and faith of his childhood; he had sought the hand of a Breton girl for this reason and constantly asked his mother and Mme Adam to seek out for him a simple Protestant girl whom he might meet and perhaps marry on returning from overseas.[1] On 20 October 1886, a few months after coming back from the Far East and before his thirty-seventh birthday, Loti married Jeanne Blanche Franc de Ferrière, who came from a fairly wealthy, Protestant family of Bordeaux and whose brother he had met in the navy in Indo-China. The couple spent their honeymoon in Spain visiting Granada and Seville and returned to live at Rochefort, where Loti continued to work in the naval administration until 6 September 1888 when he was given command of the "Ecureuil" stationed there. In May, 1887, only seven months after their marriage, Mme Loti had a miscarriage which greatly upset Loti in his desire for a descendant to ease his sense of mortality, and it was not until 18 February 1889 that she gave birth to a son, Samuel. Although his son's arrival satisfied Loti's desire for some continuity beyond death, marriage did not, however, solve his problems; in fact, it seems to have made them worse, since he saw now that he could not retrieve the simplicity, idealism, and security of his past simply by marrying someone not quite so sophisticated as himself. Only five months after his marriage Loti was complaining how depressed he was to Mme Adam[2] and noting in his diary how he disliked the changes in his life marriage had brought; and this is confirmed by the noticeable increase in his traveling abroad after it.[3] It is noticeable, for example, that he spends his first wedding anniversary searching for Aziyadé in Istanbul, is about to leave for Morocco when his son is born, and spends most of the next decade or more in the Middle East and Asia. And even when he was in France he was only occasionally seen with his wife[4]; he kept his mother company at Rochefort after his aunts' death; and his association in public with handsome sailors, whose youthful good looks and height he tried to emulate by using makeup and putting pads in his shoes, was notorious, as Goncourt reports in his *Journal.*[5] Equally well known was the decoration of his rooms in the old house at Rochefort in Turkish, Oriental, and medieval style and the fifteenth-century party he held there in April, 1888, at which Mme Adam was his leading lady and guests were requested to bring their own silver goblets and knives.[6] There was also held a *fête arabe* after Loti's return from Morocco, on 8 November 1889, to celebrate his mother's birthday, a *fête paysanne* in 1893 to inaugurate his "Breton" Room, and a "Carthaginian" *fête,* at which the actress Rose Caron came as Salammbô. He attended fancy-dress parties in society, too, and enjoyed the disguises these allowed him with a sophisticated childishness. Far from becoming simpler, Loti was encouraged by the success of his Breton novels and popularity of *Madame Chrysanthème* to indulge even more in the sophisticated and exotic in order to escape from his inability to become young, simple, and idealistic again and return to the spiritually antediluvian period of his protected childhood. Nevertheless, Loti tried to regain his past with its simplicity and faith by describing it in his works; and his desire was reflected in his naming his son after his famous Huguenot ancestor of Oleron, and in the cell-like furnishing and crucifix found in the ascetically bare bedroom he always had, and the way he conserved the old parts of the house as they were in his childhood.

II   *Carmen Silva*

Two events in 1887, both involving women, orientated Loti's thoughts toward the past in the following years. The first was Loti's acceptance of an invitation from Queen Pauline Elizabeth of Rumania to visit her at Castel Pelesh at Sinaia in the Carpathians. This had come about as the result of her secretary, Helen Vàcaresco, sending him a translation of one of the highly religious works which the Queen had published under the pseudonym of Carmen Silva;[7] Loti had read *Jéhova* and sent back in return a signed copy of *Pêcheur d'Islande,* which the Queen desired to translate—and subsequently did translate within a month! Thus, Loti found himself being met at Bucharest station on 26 September 1887 and being driven to the royal residence at Sinaia. Although he was at first a little embarrassed by people's astonishment at his small figure and shyness, Loti enjoyed his days at Sinaia, taking walks in the forested estate with members of the royal family and talking with the Queen, who insisted on reciting some of her work to him. He describes his stay with much flattery in his preface to the Queen's novel *Qui Frappe?*, (later incorporated into his work on her, *L'Exilée*) and refers to it as in "the enchanted castle of a fairy"; for the Queen had for Loti not only the snobbish attraction of being royal, but of being a "superior being" in her Christian charity and compassion for those around her; as the white hairs on her young head indicated, she had suffered much, for she too, like Loti, had recently lost a child, and her present altruism was the result of her having passed through her own personal Gethsemane and Calvary. So impressive was Carmen Silva as a person for Loti that his account of his stay at Sinaia is filled with his admiration of her and little else of the country; she represented for him both his present grief and the religious background of his youth and in this way took him back to his past. He returned to the past again, when a few days later, in early October, he left Bucharest for Varna and Istanbul on a pilgrimage to discover the fate of Aziyadé.

III   Fantôme d'Orient

As Loti writes at the opening of his account of his pilgrimage, partly written in Corsica in spring, 1891, and published in the *Nouvelle Revue* from December that year to February, 1892, he had heard no news of Hakidjé since he left Turkey and was filled with both excitement and apprehension at having a chance to discover her fate now. He confesses here too that the ending of *Aziyadé* was false and it is the real conclusion to the novel, as he later told Mme Adam,[8] that he wants to find on his two-day stay. Time has passed since he was last in Istanbul, and as he tries to evoke her memory from the few souvenirs he has of her and the faded paper with an address to which he sent his letters to her, he feels as if he is lifting the lid of the tomb of his past to find the "remains of his romance" inside; for the Loti and Aziyadé of 1876–77 are, he feels, quite dead.

Nevertheless, as soon as he enters the Bosphorus on the steamer from Varna and sees Turkish dress again, he begins to feel at home once more and is not slow on landing at Istanbul to speak Turkish to the boatmen on the quay and fix himself up with a hotel room at Pera and acquire a Greek interpreter in Galata; he manages, after a few delays, to trace at Pri-Pacha the old Armenian woman Anaktar-Chiraz, who was once an intermediary between him and Aziyadé and is now his sole contact with the past, and she introduces him to the sister of his former friend Achmed who in turn leads Loti to Kadidja, Aziyadé's former Negro maid; and it is she who guides Loti outside the city walls to the blue tombstone with gold lettering where Aziyadé lies buried just as Anaktar-Chiraz informs him where to find Achmed's pauper's grave. For Aziyadé died seven years before as the result of her being left by Loti and abandoned by her master; and Achmed and most of his family were killed during the fighting that took place after Loti's departure. The fact that these two close friends are dead, Kadidja is nearly so, and that many of the streets and buildings, such as at Eyub where he lived and the house of Abeddin-pacha where Aziyadé was kept, have been demolished makes Loti feel that the past has vanished forever; the survival, however, of certain places such as the café where he first met Achmed, the Mehmed-Faith mosque where they once sat, the Jewish market where he once wandered when he was penniless and living at Eski, and the city walls where he walked with Aziyadé reminds him of the passing of time and of the changes in his life and outlook since he was last here. He is older, rich, well known and sophisticated now, no longer the poor, lonely, adventurous lover of years ago; the mosques, alleyways, and Golden Horn remain, but along with the death of Aziyadé and Achmed something of Loti himself has died here—"something of myself lies buried in Turkish soil with Aziyadé." Hence, the sense of death and melancholy he feels in the light of the autumn sunset as he smokes his narghile at a café in a silent, deserted square and the way he embraces Aziyadé's grave. On the one hand, resigning himself to the passing of time, the ephemeralness of human life and the impassibility of Nature—symbolized here in the contrast between the changes Loti finds in Istanbul and the permanency of the old city walls and the recurrence of the sunset—Loti attempts, on the other, to regain some of what has been lost by taking home flowers from his friends' graves and clinging to his memories of them "just as one would try to hold back for a moment with one's hand something light that is floating and carried away by the current." The *fantôme d'Orient* Loti seeks is then not only the ghost of Aziyadé—and also Achmed whose death seems to cause Loti more grief than that of Aziyadé in the novel—but also the specter of his own past, which he knows is dead but wants to retrieve nonetheless. It is this that Aziyadé's Istanbul at sunset now poetically symbolizes for him; he thus sees there "living things in their association with death" in this account of his pilgrimage into a vanished past and in the novels that follow it, including *Le Roman d'un Enfant*.

IV   Le Roman d'un Enfant

This work, which Loti wrote at the request of Carmen Silva, to whom it is dedicated, and had published in the *Nouvelle Revue* from January to April, 1890, is his most famous autobiographical novel, anticipating in some respects Fournier and Proust. Briefly, it tells the story of Loti's childhood from his first memories of tottering around in the family dining room in front of the fire to the day he joined the navy; from when he is discovering the world like a young swallow fresh from the nest and his mind was as virgin and sensitive as a new photographic plate to when he begins to see into the deceptive side of life and his imagination is refined and corrupted by exotic dreams of overseas; from when the spoilt, lonely little boy is happily integrated in the traditional life of his family to when he feels nostalgically that he has left his childhood behind him and finds himself veering away from his family while still being deeply attached to them. In short, the novel attempts, as Loti does in *Fantôme d'Orient*, to "fight against the fragility of things and my own being" by trying to evoke memories of years gone by and thereby regain the past, especially the innocent, simple, spiritually idealistic days of childhood.

As can be seen from *Un Jeune Officier Pauvre*, the idea for such a novel had occurred to him as early as February, 1878, when his anguish in the Trappist monastery first made him conscious of his break with the past. Since most of the work was not, however, written until Loti was nearly forty years old, his view of his childhood is necessarily biased by his outlook of 1890. As was seen in

Chapter 1, he is extremely sentimental and nostalgic in his early
impressions of his mother's protective affection for him, of his love
of the traditional faith of Oleron, and his infatuation with the
natural wonders of Limoise and the insects and flowers of the Rochefort countryside and the Midi. But at the same time his brother's influence, his reading of books on foreign parts, and his collections of
exotic objects cause his mind to stray from the traditional values of
his home and wander far from his studies at school; and he begins to
cultivate the fetishistic practice of evoking the past and overseas by
association with old or exotic objects he has at home. Thus, he
makes a habit of continually contrasting past and present, here and
elsewhere, which will open a rift both in his outlook on life and in
his personality, and is reflected not only in the novel's vain nostalgia for the past, but also in its evocation of sensations in the past
to convey the author's mood and thoughts of the present. In the same
way as his playing with Lucette and Véronique, his rushing out of
school to show his parents the colorful moths of the countryside,
the sound of the muffin woman and many other incidents which
he enjoys recalling evoke his childhood happiness at home, the story
of the little boy who loses his family and visits his home now they
are gone, the pond his brother builds for him before he goes away
never to return, the disillusionment of springtime and the unanswered
prayers of the schoolgirls he sees at Rochefort illustrate for him at
present the ephemeralness of all things, the fragility of human
existence, the deceptions of life, and the absence of God; and the
evocativeness of his exotic butterfly collection on summer evenings
long ago conveys his present urge to leave home for overseas just
as the autumn melancholy, which is juxtaposed with the idyllic
enjoyment of warm summers throughout the novel and particularly
at the end, implies in retrospect the fading of Loti's childhood in
this "song of years gone by and summer days that have long since
passed away."

It is this adult attitude of sentimentality and melancholy toward
childhood—seen in his allusions to fairy stories in his other works—
and the consequent false simplicity of Loti's point of view that lend
the novel its charm; the scenes of two little infants drawing together
by the fireside, of the child's mother sitting tenderly at his bedside,
or of the young boy exploring the garden and countryside, Oleron
or Castelnau, are, however, charming precisely because they are

described through the older, aesthetically refined eye of the nostalgic, middle-aged Loti: the adult writer can exploit retrospectively his memories of a distant past with the same detached desire for impressionistic and realistic immediacy in his evocation of childhood sensations as when he evokes faraway places on his return to France or Brittany in the Far East. The false simplicity or sophisticated childishness of *Le Roman d'un Enfant* reflects, then, Loti's intention to somehow join together through the immediacy of his autobiographical writing his past and present selves as a bulwark against the ravages of time and death.

V Matelot

If *Le Roman d'un Enfant* revives for Loti his nostalgia for the days of Limoise and Oleron, *Matelot,* which was published in 1893, dedicated to Queen Marie-Christine of Spain, may be said to evoke his memories of the years following the close of the earlier work. Unlike the autobiographical *Roman d'un Enfant,* this novel is partly fictional and partly biographical, the latter element being composed of details from the lives of both Loti and his close, handsome sailor friend Léo Thémèze,[9] for whom he had gained a post first on the "Ecureuil" and later in a merchant shipping company. Just as Loti fused the experiences of himself and his big brother or his more virile friends in his early novels, so he now personalizes some of Léo's early life and physical appearance in his plot. Young Jean Berny, like Loti himself, dreams of faraway places, and his reading of exotic literature urges him to join the navy; his failing the entrance examination for the *Borda* and the decline of his family's finances cause Jean, like Léo, to join the navy as a sailor; Jean and his mother, like Loti and Mme Viaud at Rochefort, live together in a small, fairly cheap lodging in Brest after being forced to move from their comfortable old home in the Midi; unfortunately, Jean, like Gustave Viaud, contracts anemia in Indo-China and is buried at sea during his stormy journey home.

Jean is a tragic figure: a victim of his own temperament and of fate; and his tragic development is based on a series of shots of him at different stages of his life and emphasized by repeated references back in time to the first few of these. The novel opens with seven-year-old Jean looking very innocent and devoted as an

"angelic choirboy" in a Corpus Christi procession in Provence;
despite his family's financial worries and his mother's fears of her
son growing up, little Jean is happy in his new Easter suit sitting
at the dinner table at home; as the circling swallows and bats he
watches from the twilit schoolhouse signify, young Jean has all
of life as well as all of the Easter holidays before him; his outlook is
one of innocent idealism. The next shot of him at seventeen at
the time of his failing his examination and joining up as a sailor
shows him dreaming of India and Egypt. Owing to the financial
difficulties of the family, he realizes that his course will not be easy
and that the carefree happiness of his childhood is gone. In fact, he
already looks back nostalgically to the Eastertime of ten years
earlier and has "an early premonition of life's inevitable twilight
and end." This feeling of regret for the past is confirmed when, after
a short period of enjoyable physical exercise as a sailor on board ship
and a tempting glimpse of an Oriental beauty at Rhodes, Jean
returns home to find his mother about to move house. An autumn
atmosphere replaces the spring one of years ago; and when they
finally leave, they take with them little Jean's Corpus Christi outfit and some pressed flowers from their garden as mementos of a
vanishing past and slam the doors shut like "the lids on a tomb."
The days of Jean's childhood and the family's traditional happiness
are over, as is denoted by the dark beard and bronzed skin that now
surround Jean's childishly candid eyes and the contrast in climate and
surroundings between Antibes and Brest; they must rely on the few
relics of the past they have brought with them to evoke memories
of happier times, when Jean was not so attracted to the exotic by his
reading and circumstances had not encouraged him further to leave
home and go overseas—a theme reflected in the failure of Jean's
platonic relationship with Madeleine, a Breton girl he meets when on
leave in Brest. Jean's volunteering to serve in Indo-China is the
final stage in "the fatality of which he is unaware"; his weakness at
the end of a year in the swamplands, his removal to the *mouroir*
on board the "Saône," his delirium as the ship sways and rolls,
his longing to write to and see his mother, his memories of the past,
and his slow agony during a storm bring Jean's story to a tragic
close, symbolized in the quick, crude funeral he is given and the
smashing of his improvised coffin beneath the ship.

The reader has been aware throughout the novel of Jean's cruel destiny by the allusions of fate and death and a reference to his burial at sea after the failure of his romance with Madeleine, but Mme Berny does not know of her son's death until it is revealed to her by Jean's sailor friends when the ship enters port. In this way, Loti builds up the pathos of the situation as he describes her preparing for Jean's return and dressing herself to meet him at the ship and manages to convey the full impact of the shock on her; at first, she wants to kill herself and is almost demented; gradually, however, she resigns herself to this blow of fate and eventually, like the sailors who pray on board ship as the ominous albatrosses circle overhead, she finds consolation in religious worship and hopes of an after-life, clinging with Loti's fetishism to a certain Corpus Christi outfit as a relic of an Eastertime long ago.

VI   Le Livre de la Pitié et de la Mort

Matelot closes with Loti praising God for providing the solace of prayer and an afterlife to those confronted with death or in distress, even though he himself is no longer a believer: "And we who have lost You forever, let us kiss amid our tears the footprint You left behind in the dust as You took leave of us . . . " *Le Livre de la Pitié et de la Mort,* published in July, 1890, and dedicated to Mme Viaud because she has faith and can therefore resign herself to such horrors as death, shows us Loti taking refuge in a desire for compassion for this fate of all men and all creatures as a substitute for faith. The compassion he tried to evoke by the artistry of his writing was non-altruistic and really an exteriorization of his own self-pity just as his descriptions of the exotic were symbolically evocative of his attitude to life. In *Le Livre de la Pitié et de la Mort* there are several examples of this pity for the distressed and dying, whether they are human or animal; *L'Oeuvre de Pen-Bron* describes Loti's visit to the hospital for spastics and cripples on Pen-Bron; *Veuves de Pêcheurs* is part of Loti's public appeal for a fund to help the widows of shipwrecked Breton fishermen; *Chagrin d'un Vieux Forçat* is a tale once told to Loti by "Yves" of a convict's attachment to a little caged bird which eventually dies at sea to the grief of the old criminal and evokes a Hugolian pity for both convict and bird; *Une Bête Galeuse* tells of how Loti and his servant Sylvestre put a mangy cat out of its misery, and *Viande de Boucherie* similarly evokes pity for animals in their confrontation with death—in this case, bullocks about to be slaughtered for meat on board ship; and *Vie de Deux Chattes* describes the pleasure Loti's two cats gave him and the sadness of their sudden death, which anticipated almost the passing of his aunt Clarisse in December, 1890, realistically and sentimentally conveyed in *Tante Claire nous quitte*. His aunt's prolonged agony in her struggle with death, compared by Loti to a moth through which someone has stuck a needle,[10] and her extinction amid all the things that recall for Loti her part in his childhood evoke his pity for her and his sentimental attachment to all he associates with her.

VII *L'Exilée*

A final example of Loti's evocation of pity for others in their confrontation with distress and death is his account, published in 1893, of his meeting with the virtually exiled Carmen Silva at the Hotel Danieli in Venice in August, 1891. Already on his second short visit to Bucharest in April, 1890, Loti had felt amid the celebrations for the Queen's birthday, denoted by the flower decorations and dances in national costume, that there was something troubling the Queen's mind and an atmosphere of latent mistrust in her entourage. By 1891 all of Europe knew through the sensational reporting of the press that the Queen had incurred the King's displeasure by encouraging the romance between the young heir to the throne and her secretary, Helen Vacaresco; the fact that the Queen had moved to Venice was interpreted as a voluntary exile.

When Loti visited her there,[11] he found her writing what appeared to be her last religious work and much deteriorated in health; and his depiction of her pale, sad appearance which she tried to hide by the activity of her fertile mind and her writing her *Livre de l'Ame* matches his description of the morbidly grey dawn over Venice with its stagnant canals, black gondolas and Bridge of Sighs, and the charm of the city reflected at night in the water.[12] When the Queen's party goes out in a gondola and the Queen, weak and exhausted, reads aloud from her *Livre de l'Ame* against the symbolic background of a Venetian sunset and assumes an air of supreme serenity in the face of her illness and exile, Loti calls the Christian ethic "the most radiant of mirages" in its relief of suffering and expresses "a vast, deeply felt compassion" for the dying exile. Carmen Silva symbolizes in her resignation to suffering and compassion for others as well as in her charity toward her entourage the active virtues of Christianity; it is the faith and consolation of these, as opposed to his own detached evocation of pity, and the security of childhood which Loti was seeking in his remembrance of a simple, vanished past as a refuge against the changes wrought by time and death in his own physical and spiritual being and in the world around him.

CHAPTER 6

The Quest for Lost Faith

I *Loti's Later Development*

BY the late 1880's and early 1890's when *Roman d'un Enfant,*
Fantôme d'Orient, Matelot, and *Livre de la Pitié et de la*
Mort appeared, Loti was acutely aware that he might never be able
to regain his former simplicity and faith. When in Paris on one of his
infrequent flying visits, he would stay at the modest Hotel Bon
Lafontaine under the name of Monsieur Daniel so as to avoid
publicity and dine at Princess Bibesco's, Countess Diane de Beau-
secq's, the d'Haussonvilles and Halévy's. Many of his friends were
sensitive aesthetes and literary dilettantes such as Jean Thorel, Louis
de Robert, and Prince Bojidar Karageorgevitch. His election to
the Académie Française[1] on 21 May 1891 to replace Octave
Feuillet merely confirmed his sophisticated role as a literary celeb-
rity of the period. His awareness of this, his paternity, the loss of
his childhood aunts, and his visits to Carmen Silva made him,
however, extremely conscious in his lack of belief of the passing of
time and his aging and increasingly anguished in his reflections on
death. Nevertheless, he did not stop trying to find some belief in
eternity, which would allow him to escape the utter annihilation of
death and console him in his loss of the past and of the family of his
childhood; and his works become largely travelogues of pilgrimages
through unspoilt Nature, dominated by this skeptical moral quest
for childhood simplicity and faith and set in an anguished spiritual
context in which metaphors of decline and death loom largest.

The image of the increasingly desperate neo-Bedouin pilgrim thus
replaces that of the ideal lover of *Aziyadé* in the exotic cult of
himself Loti created to hide his ever greater insecurity outside the
company of his mother and close sailor friends. Instead of painting
his work in the exotic colors of some symbolically idealized romance
or friendship with the intimate details of local life such a relationship gave insight into, Loti now stresses his anguish rather than his
idealism, and describes the scenes before him with less poetic exteri-

orization of his ideas in exotic settings and more direct reference to
the moral value of the experiences of his quest. Each of his visits
overseas is now more visibly the subject of a moral experience rather
than the stimulant of aesthetic sensations with moral implications.
Lafcadio Hearn admirably described Loti's development when he
wrote:

> To me Loti seems for a space to have looked into Nature's whole splendid,
> burning, fulgurant soul . . . He was young. Then the color and the light
> faded and only the worn-out blasé nerves remained; and the poet became—
> a little, morbid, modern, affected Frenchman.[2]

Although Loti's style does not alter noticeably and is still dominated by the concisely detailed realism and impressionistic immediacy of his roving viewpoint, it is natural that as his work became
more moral and less sensational, so his message became
more important than his evocation of the exotic. Whereas he was
able before to hide the calculated structure of his prose beneath the
smooth dynamism of his intimate impressions, now the required
selection of scenes becomes more evident; the author's direct intervention is more frequent; and, as Henry James was to comment,[3]
the reader occasionally hears the tick of the mechanism controlling
the perfect pointing of the watch of Loti's narrative.

II   Au Maroc

On 19 March 1889 Loti obtained two months' leave from his
post on the "Ecureuil" at Rochefort to accompany J. Patenôtre,
French minister at Tangier, down to Fez to present his letters of
credence to the Sultan; Patenôtre[4] chose Loti to represent
the French navy and four officers to represent the army in his and
the government's desire to impress the Sultan with French prestige
and power. Loti's departure on such an official mission and on so
dangerous an expedition into a wild country still ravaged by tribal
wars and brigands caused quite a sensation in the European press
and became almost an event of world importance.[5] He left
Marseilles on board the "Cettori" on 16 March for Tangier, where
he arrived nine days later. An account of his journey from 4 April
to 4 May down to Fez and Meknes and back again appeared in
Au Maroc, first published in *L'Illustration* from August to
October, 1889.

As Loti's preface makes clear, his account is not concerned with the politics nor the court and harem life of the Sultan, but with the traditionalism of Islamic culture based on unspoilt simplicity, age-old faith and aesthetic indulgence and epitomized by the Sultan's outlook. *Au Maroc* is then not merely a day-by-day account of Loti's setting out on 4 April with a small train of donkeys, camels, and Bedouin porters from Tangier into the heart of the Magrab empire; of the various tribes they have as escorts on their daily progress under the red banner of the Sultan; of the vast *mounas* or offerings of food they receive from sheiks along their route and live sacrifices they are brought by local plaintiffs; of the changes in the landscape from bare scrubland and rocky foothills to green fields of corn and flowers and palm and olive groves flanked by the snowcapped Atlas mountains under skies, now dazzling with sunlight, now dark with rain; of their crossing of the swollen Oued-M'cazen, Lecoutz, and Sebon Rivers and the camps they set up in fields, cemeteries, and outside the gray city walls of Fez and Meknes; of their grand reception by the sheriff of Czar-el-Kehir in his tranquil residence and having tea in the orange groves of Caïd Abassi of the Beni-Malek tribe's gardens; of their visiting the vast market of Seguelda, where everything from live-stock and spices to saddles and water are sold to hundreds of tribesmen from miles around, the covered bazar of Fez, where each trade and craft is established in separate sectors and races from all over Africa meet and bargain, and the beggars' market and richly decorated Jewish quarter of Meknes; and of their stay in the strictly Moslem cities of the Sultanate—their entertainment by various vizirs in Moorish surroundings of mosaic tiling and fountains, their audience and exchange of gifts with the Sultan himself, and Loti's exploring the sinister alleyways of Fez dressed in Arab garb. *Au Maroc* is also, as the preface implies, a defense of Islam in Morocco. Loti likes the open-air life under tents amid the primitive simplicity of Nature and the fierceness of the tribal escorts who display their skills, their horses, their guns, and the gold and silk of their saddles and burnous in fantastic cavalcades and bouts of shooting along their route; they recall for him with his delight in poetic romanticizing the great days of Mahomet's fanatical wars for the promulgation of Islam and reflect its unspoilt state. The caïds of the El-Araïch and Beni-Hassem tribes look like the

Prophet, the hundreds of people at Seguelda market recall the masses who followed the prophets of the Old Testament and Koran, and the difficult crossing of the Oued-M'cazen River with men swimming and camels and mules being hauled up the slippery banks evokes for him a scene from one of Mahomet's campaigns. Although a little disturbed by the discomfort and isolation of his lodgings in Fez-bali—which he acquired from Dr. Linarès, one of the few Christians resident in the city—and by the cruelty of the slave market and "salt" punishment for robbers, Loti admires the steadfastness with which the Moroccans adhere to their traditional culture and faith in their attitude to Christian infidels and Western influences; he shares the Islamic love of gardens, perfumes, veiled women, mosaic-tiled courtyards and mosques, and beautiful carpets; and he enjoys the immobility and hope of eternity of Islam and remarks on the nonchalant manner and inspired look of the people in the bazaar at Fez, for he too likes to dream on the terrace of his lodgings at sunset and peer down at the women cautiously eying him there, and he too desires that hope of eternity after death.

But the independence and integrity of Islam is threatened now by infiltration from the West as well as by its own gradual decline; the thick gray walls surrounding Fez and Meknes are silent and crumbling slowly, the gardens of the Sultan like the Aguedal gardens in Meknes are overgrown, the Sultan himself is old and as if mummified in the shroud of his white burnous, the next generation represented by the vizir's sons are pale and weary from inactivity, and the muezzin's chant at sunset seems to announce the imminent decline of that original vitality of Mahomet which brought Islam to the Magrab. *Au Maroc* thus closes with Loti's urgent plea to Allah to preserve Morocco and Islam's primitive vitality and faith and save these and the related, unspoilt freedom of the countryside from the turmoil and innovations of the West epitomized on their return in the refined tourists and comfortable hotels of Tangier, which they reach on 5 May. Loti's journey to Fez reflected for him the traditionalism and faith of the past he longed for and the primitive vitality of Nature he enjoyed; the decline of Islam in the Magrab in the face of the advent of Western civilization evokes in him, then, the melancholy of his own vanished past of belief and simplicity.

III   Le Désert

After his return from Morocco, Loti spent some more time on the "Ecureuil" at Rochefort until 23 September 1890; then on the "Formidable" cruising in the Mediterranean from 23 January to 1 October 1891 and on the "Courbet," mainly at Toulon, from 1 October to 22 November 1891; finally he was placed in command of the "Javelot" on the Bidassoa near Hendaye on 16 December 1891; this post he held with a period of leave from 16 June 1893 to 16 May 1896, when he served in the administration of the Rochefort Prefecture Maritime and visited the Middle East, until 1 January 1898. In between coastal patrols Loti continued to write *L'Exilée* and *Matelot* and to attend in Paris rehearsals of his dramatized works and meetings of the Académie, of which he was now a member, having made his official entry with a tribute to Feuillet on 4 April 1892. On 4 February 1894 Loti took leave from the Prefecture Maritime and left France with Léo Thémèze, his close, handsome sailor friend, and the Duke of Tallyrand-Périgord, whom Mme Adam had sent along, for Cairo and Suez, whence they were to cross the desert to Akaba, Sinai, Gaza, and finally Jerusalem.

The object of this dangerous trek across the Arabian Petraean desert with its savage, rebellious tribes, cutthroat brigands and lack of water was to prepare Loti for his pilgrimage to the Holy Land; he hoped to find in its solitude and natural primitiveness some spiritual stimulation for the childhood faith he clearly wished to revive by his visit to Palestine, just as in Morocco he had appreciated Islam by being among the tribesmen in their natural element; in short, he was trying to lose some of his late nineteenth-century French veneer of sophistication and skepticism and, by immersing himself in the primitive simplicity and vitality of the Bedouin and Nature, come nearer to the understanding of Christ's original appeal and message he had had in childhood.[6] His account of his journey through the desert from Suez to Gaza is given in *Le Désert,* first published in the *Nouvelle Revue* from September to December, 1894.

Apart from a brief halt because of cold and snow at the ancient convent built by Justinian on the slopes of Mount Sinai and an even briefer stop at the Turkish outpost of Akaba to get a safe-conduct to Gaza from Mohammed-Jahl, a desert sheik, Loti's account of his trek is filled with descriptions of the desert landscape: first, the gray-yellow sands studded with mica pebbles and the odd juniper or palm grove of the Nubian desert; then, the boulders of pink and green granite surrounded by aromatic plants and the oddly-shaped peaks of the Sinaian plateau; the pink granite rocks crumbling into ash-gray sand of the vast corridors of the Djebel-Tih gorges; the shell-covered, pinkish shores of the Gulf of Akaba set against the dark blue of the sea and the dazzling brilliance of the sky; the gray plateau covered in fossils of Arabia Petraea with its undulating sand dunes specked with black onyx, its occasional juniper, thorn-bush, gazelle and stork, and its watery mirages; and finally, the scrubland of Cedar and the barley fields and flowers of Canaan. To Loti's poetic eye the desert landscape "has the splendor of unchanging matter free of all that is unstable in life, the geological splendor of before the Creation"; it reflects the primitiveness he seeks. The mountains of Sinai and gorges of Djebel-Tin remind him of the turmoil of Creation and the mountain peaks from Akaba look as if they belong to some primeval chaos; the silence and im-mobility of the open expanses of desert occasionally fill him with anxiety and melancholy, a desire to be elsewhere and out of danger, but more often enchant him by their natural state and their fresh air "as virginal as before the Creation." The ragged Bedouin who accompany Loti and his companions with some twenty camels carrying their tents and provisions similarly remind Loti of primitive man in their wildness when they wrangle over pay and provisions and impress him by their idyllic simplicity when they sing at night around their fire in the middle of the sandy expanse. It is for this reason that Loti enjoyed so much being in Bedouin dress and on a camel during this trek; it confirmed the impressions of primitive simplicity he wanted to receive in his experiences of desert life.

It is no coincidence that when Loti and his friends seek refuge in the convent on Mount Sinai and visit the Crypt of the Burning Bush, the young monk who sees to the menial tasks of the convent and acts as their guide amid the priceless relics, icons, and manuscripts of the Byzantine chapels, appears to him like the young Christ "humbly devoted to human needs among things so ancient that they too encourage this impression of a scene from His life." The apparent resemblance anticipates the humble, simple Christ Loti wished to evoke in his visit to Jerusalem, for which his forty days of

wandering in the primitive world of the desert had been, as in the
life of the Savior Himself, a sort of purgatorial, spiritual pre-
paration.

IV Jérusalem

On 26 March 1894, Loti and his companions leave their camels
and the desert behind and set out from Gaza on mules through
pastoral countryside dotted with olive groves and vineyards for
Hebron, Bethlehem, and Jerusalem. As Loti's preface to his account
of his pilgrimage, published in the *Nouvelle Revue* from December,
1894 to March, 1895, explains, he came to Jerusalem in the hope
of regaining some belief in the Christian promise of eternal life as a
protection against the annihilation of death; he came like so many
sophisticated souls of the nineteenth century who had lost the
simplicity and faith of their youth and "although not believing,
came nevertheless to the Holy Sepulchre with a prayer in their heart
and tears in their eyes"; Loti's account of his visit is, then, not only
a description of his impressions of the Holy Places, but a diary
"written in a great desire to be sincere" of his "uncertain, desperate
adoration" of them. For Loti, Jerusalem and Palestine are, as his
first chapter heading suggests, the *spes unica,* and everywhere he
goes he tries to evoke poetically in his mind scenes and characters
from the Bible so as to make some sort of human contact with the
Judaic and Christian past in place of the faith he does not have. At
Hebron he peers through a hole in the huge stones covering Abraham's
tomb and later imagines Abraham to have resembled one of the
village chiefs of the surrounding Beit-Djinbrin valley, which evokes
for him "the pastoral life of long ago . . . the days of the Bible in
all their simplicity and grandeur." When they camp by the massive
ruins of Solomon's summer palace outside Bethlehem, after their
visit to the Church of the Nativity, Loti reflects how little the landscape of pastoral scenes and the mountains of Moab before him have
changed since Christ's time, and imagines one of the passing village
women as the Madonna with the infant Jesus in her arms:

A few yards away from us, she stops and leans on the trunk of an olive tree,
her gaze lowered in the serene and lovely manner of the Madonna: She
is a very young woman with pure features, dressed in blue and pink under
a veil with long white folds in it. Other saintly-looking women follow her,
noble and serene in their flowing dresses and also wearing a hennin and

veil; they form thus an ideal group, which the setting sun surrounds with a
halo in a last glimmer of light; they speak and smile with our humble
muleteers, wishing to offer us the water in their amphora and the oranges
in their baskets.

As with his other exoticism, the scenes he describes in the Holy Land
are romanticized exteriorizations of his own ideas and mood—
here, of a nostalgic desire for simple faith symbolized in the profile
of the peasant Madonna in the sunset glow. Similarly, in Jerusalem
Loti visits the Holy Sepulchre, El-Aksa mosque, and the Wailing
Wall, but he is above all impressed by the Roman pavement the
Daughters of Zion show him among their excavations and the
threshold of the city gate leading to Golgotha to which the Domi-
nicans lead him along the Via Dolorosa; for these remains allow
him to imagine the crucifixion in human terms of the suffering and
tears of Christ and his family amid the everyday indifference of the
Jewish population of the time; and he remarks: "never had I felt
so close on a human level to Christ the man and friend of us all"
because of the emotive force of these "human associations."

But despite these imaginative gropings toward a human understanding of Christ and the Virgin Mary in his desire—as in *Matelot*—
for their consolation and promise of eternity, Loti cannot find
enough faith here to be convinced again of the Christian message.
Hence his annoyance with the thousands of tourists who come by
boat and train, Baedeker in hand, filled with dilettantist curiosity
and carefree merriment, to invade the Holy Places with their hordes;
and his irritation at the way the monks have prostituted themselves to the tourists and souvenir hunters. He regrets now he ever set
foot in Bethlehem and spoilt the illusions he had about it; he is
saddened at seeing Jerusalem exploited by so many unthinking
tourists and becoming like any other city in Europe; he is vexed
after his trek across the desert at coming across so many noisy,
singing visitors being driven in comfortable carriages on asphalt
roads through the peaceful biblical countryside where Christ once
walked. Furthermore, he dislikes the idolatry and pomp with which
Christ is worshiped by the various churches in the Holy Sepulchre,
particularly when he is shown the rich treasures of the Roman,
Greek, and Armenian churches and sees the splendid robes and
mitres of the Coptic sect in the Byzantine chapel of St. Helen;

their conception and worship of Christ is too far from the original humble man of faith and the simplicity of early Christianity for Loti with his Protestant background "enlightened by the pure Testaments," even though he knows he should not disdain the love of ornamentation of the poor and simple whom Christ cherished among his followers. With the influx of tourists and the stress on idolatry of the churches, Loti feels that the true Christian message has been corrupted and the Holy Places will never again have the religious significance they once had.

With these views, it is not surprising that Loti's nocturnal visit, with an armed guard for protection, to the Garden of Gethsemane and his prostration on the ground are no possible help in his search for faith and only leave him in "the greatest void of all" with "my soul frustrated once more and deprived of faith forever"; and that his second visit to Golgotha and desire to imitate the Russian pilgrims there in their worship of the rock should end in tears of frustration and despair: frustration at not being able to have faith either through an emotional commitment or even a rational need to somehow understand the enigma of Christ and the universe; and despair at not finding a way to the consolation and afterlife of Christ and still being faced with the decay of death which he detects in the moribund pilgrims around him, and ultimate annihilation such as he finds in the Valley of Jehoshafat and the ruins he has visited during his stay in Jerusalem. The sense of "the nothingness of Man, the passing of all civilizations and nations" that he feels among the ruins of particularly the Omar mosque and of ancient Jericho reflects Loti's failure to rediscover his faith. Loti's account closes with an appeal to others like himself to seek Christ as he has done even if they too only find Him for a brief second, for there is no other hope to rescue men from the annihilation of death.[7]

V   La Galilée

This third and final part of Loti's account of his pilgrimage to Palestine, dedicated to Léo Thémèze, is the most somber and pedantic of the series; not because the itinerary itself from Jerusalem through Bethel, Nablus, Nazareth, Tiberias, Caesarea, and Damascus to Beirut is unattractive or the landscape of barley fields, scrubland, mountains—Gilboa, Tabor, Hittim, Hermon—and

Jordan swamps under a rainy sky is unappealing; but because Loti tries to describe "mournful Galilee" as "silent under a vast shroud of flowers" and show that it is now after the ravages of history a silent, desolate land where only nature still flourishes among the ruins. In order to impress on the reader this consciousness of a vanished past of civilizations and battles, Loti refers all he sees to incidents in the Bible and history: The dolmens he remarks on during his stay with the Samaritans at Mt. Garizim are alluded to in Deuteronomy; the columns the guide shows him in Samaria date back to the time of Herod and Jezebel; the mountains they pass evoke a host of biblical references as well as the Crusades and Napoleon's campaigns; and the ruins of Tell-Houm on Tiberias, of Lesem-Dan near Lake Houleh and of Damascus and Baalbek call forth concise but still rather tedious paragraphs on their historical origins. All the great cities of Christ's day are now little more than crumbling ruins or Arab hamlets; there is a "melancholy of abandonment" on the slopes of Mt. Hermon so rich in history; Tiberias is like Pompeii a "silent land of some sleeping Beauty whom it is too late to awaken"; a "deathly hush hangs over this cradle of civilization," where Capernaum, Bethsaida, and Magdala once stood and Christ drew vast crowds of villagers and fishermen; the ruins from His day are now used by Bedouin nomads for shelter and overgrown with a "shroud of greenery"; and only the occasional woman comes to draw water or clean some fish on the lake's silent shores where the Christian message was first proclaimed.

For Loti the mortal silence and overgrown state of Galilee reflect his failure to retrieve his faith and the decline of Christ's original message of love and eternity in the modern world. At Nazareth, as at Tiberias, Loti is able to imagine the young Christ gazing out over the unchanging landscape and is inspired with a sense of religious awe, but this soon vanishes when he is shown the touristic attractions of Christ's birthplace and sees the crowds of tourists at Damascus, for whom the new railway from Beirut is being built and who scrawl their names over the gigantic columns at Baalbek. After marveling at these "Titanesque constructions," which symbolize Man's concern with religion from the earliest times and suggest in their present melancholy futility and exploitation by tourists the fate of the other ruins he has seen in Palestine, Loti realizes more than ever the fragility of all human activity and despairs even more of the decline of the East under Western influence, as in Morocco, and of the sacred past it has preserved for so long. Loti is saddened by the failure of his pilgrimage to regain the simplicity and faith he sought and the advent of Western civilization with its skepticism and sophistication to the Middle East only makes him fear the future and death with even more dread and anguish.

VI   Ramuntcho

The failure of Loti's pilgrimage to the Holy Land left him with an even greater anguish and despair at ever regaining simplicity and faith than before he embarked on it. In late May, 1894, he returned via Smyrna and Istanbul to Rochefort and the Prefecture Maritime, acutely conscious of his inevitable aging and the increasing prospect of death without the solace of faith now that he was approaching middle age and his mother was in her early eighties. His sense of anguished despair is conveyed in his famous novel on the Basque country, *Ramuntcho,* which he began at Rochefort on 1 November 1893, prompted by the nostalgia and melancholy his mother's eighty-third birthday evoked in him; the novel was completed at Ascain, near Hendaye, on 8 November 1896, after he had resumed command of the "Javelot", and published in the *Revue de Paris* from 15 December 1896 to 15 February 1897; the novel's composition[8] thus spans Loti's visit to Palestine and reflects the feelings this provoked in him.

According to the novel's dedication to Loti's neighbor at Hendaye, Mme D'Abbadia, he became initiated into Basque life in late 1891, when he was given command of the "Javelot" and began to live in the house rented from Dr. Durruty, which he was to buy in 1904 and call Bakhar-Etchea, the House of the Solitary. He soon began to join in the smuggling trips across the French-Spanish border of his friend Otharré Borda of Ascain and to play *pelota* there with the local villagers in an effort to revive his own vitality and belief by indulging in the primitive pleasures and age-old traditions of this isolated race, which had its own strange language and customs and reminded him of Brittany, and no doubt Oleron, in its innocent simplicity and faith. By June, 1893, he already refers to it as "my part of the country";[9] he enjoys watching his blond sailor friend

Joseph Brahy leaping about the unspoilt green countryside of trees and mountains like a young savage; he admires the primitive virility of the men playing *pelota* and smuggling silk, velvet, phosphorus, or copper across the border by night; he is attracted to the Basque women as they sing and dance the sensuous fandango; and he is impressed by the church masses and wayside crucifixes which play such a vital part in the life of this primitive people isolated within a virtually antediluvian countryside. He wrote in his diary in 1893:

Everywhere there is the healthy peacefulness of a rustic existence whose traditions down here in the Basque country are more static than anywhere else. And at all the crossroads, in the vast penumbra cast over everything by the trees, the heavy clouds, and the high Pyrenees hidden behind them— everywhere, there are old crucifixes with the sublime but simple message on them, which might be taken as the motto of the Basque people: *O crux, ave spes unica!*[10]

Ramuntcho is Loti's tribute to the Basque's primitive and traditional life and a confession of his own despairing sense of irrevocable alienation from such an existence.

The novel's plot of Ramuntcho's love for Gracieuse and of her withdrawal into a convent was based on an actual romance of which Loti heard from local villagers. His impressions of Basque life—the episodes relating to smuggling, *pelota,* the fandango, and the villages around the Bidassoa and Nivelle Rivers—were drawn with slight alterations from his *journal intime* just as his description of the convent derives from his own visit with Otharré to see the latter's sister in a nunnery at Méharin;[11] only the original names were changed—Otharré and Brahy become Arrochkoa, Méharin is Amezqueta, Ascain is called Etchezar, for example—and the ending of Ramuntcho's inability to abduct Gracieuse from the convent and departure for America were contrived to give the novel the meaning Loti wanted it to convey.

Ramuntcho represents to some extent in the novel the Basque race as Loti saw it; the opening scene showing him singing a Basque song as he returns to his simple home on a rainy autumn evening through the now golden countryside reveals at once the youthful muscular agility and virility he has of primitive Man as he deftly picks his way through the fields just as his silent nimbleness in his cord shoes

indicates already the cautious step of the smuggler. At seventeen
years of age, he has the physique of a man and the innocence of a
child; like his tough, athletic friends Itchoua, Arrochkoa, and
Florentino, Ramuntcho enjoys the primitive pleasures of stealth
and risk of their smuggling expeditions, epitomized in the savage-
like *irrintzina* or victory cry given on their return, for they are,
according to Loti's romanticized view of simple folk's natural
vitality, "a reminder of Man's most primitive sensations in the jungles
and forests of prehistoric times." Like them, too, he likes drinking
cider in an inn in the evening and playing *pelota* in the church
square in the afternoon; and despite these wilder activities, he will
attend with the other villagers Sunday and Saints-day masses at the
Spanish Renaissance-style church with its separate pews for men
and women and Basque tombstones, and continue in the traditional faith of his race as a solace against the passing of time and
death.

Ramuntcho also shows himself to be representatively Basque in his
romance with Gracieuse, whom he has already known for five years:
Loti depicts the natural development of the couple's love through
events in the traditional life of the village and the effect of seasonal
changes in the wild countryside. Their first meeting in the novel
takes place after the All Saints Day mass and is quite idyllic
and chaste; their second one is at the *pelota* match later that day
when Ramuntcho shows off his strength and virility while Gracieuse
admiringly looks after his shirt and wicker glove; the next one is
at the fandango dancing that evening when, silently and without
any contact between them, Gracieuse's sensuous swaying of her hips
arouses as yet innocent desires in her partner as he snaps his
fingers to the beat of her movements. When early spring comes and
the trees and countryside turn green once more, Ramuntcho's desire
for Gracieuse increases—symbolized in the noises he hears of the
cattle and horses in the sheds near his bedroom—and the couple meet
secretly in the evenings. It is not, however, until they meet at Er-
ribiague, where Ramuntcho has come to play *pelota*, that they
kiss for the first time—the pleasure of his sensual biting of her lips and
her licking of his nascent moustache being erotically symbolized in
their visit soon after to the cherry orchards and the blooming of the
countryside under the May rains. As the summer heat arrives and
the Basques indulge in more smuggling, more *pelota* matches, and

more fandango dancing, Ramuntcho yearns more and more to possess
Gracieuse at their nightly meetings.

Two sets of circumstances, however, prevent their marriage:
first, the refusal of Gracieuse's mother to let her marry Ramuntcho
and her postponement of their marriage until they are of age
and he has completed his military service; and secondly, her withdrawal into the convent of Ste Marie du Rosaire under pressure
from her mother, while he is away, and the impossibility of their
ever resuming their former relations when he returns. Throughout
the novel Gracieuse associates with the sisters of Ste Marie du
Rosaire and, when her romance with Ramuntcho develops, a conflict begins within her between terrestrial pleasures and celestial
ecstasy, the turmoil of human love and the calm of spiritual bliss
when she enters the village church; this is symbolized in her buying
the picture of the Virgin on their journey to the Valley of the Cherries.
When her mother's actions prevent her enjoyment of the pleasures
of this life, she then quite naturally falls back on the comfort and joy
the Church affords and gives herself up completely to that spiritual
inheritance of the Basque people.

While Gracieuse returns to the sources of Basque traditionalism,
Ramuntcho departs from it. As the illegitimate child[12] of his
mother's liaison with a sophisticated Frenchman from the city,
Ramuntcho has the more refined sensibility and desire for change
and being elsewhere, already seen in the subject of *Matelot,* and
the anguished lack of belief which permeates Loti's work. Ramuntcho's Basque qualities mentioned earlier lend him the primitive simplicity and adherence to tradition Loti associated with his childhood,
while his sense of spiritual and aesthetic detachment from the simple
life of his people and his consequent desire for change and "elsewhere"—which his reading and military service overseas only encourage—were the problems of Loti and his generation in the mid-1890's.
When soon after his return home his mother dies, Ramuntcho has
no longer any ties with the village, now that Gracieuse is in the convent; the Easter bells have long had no meaning for him; he cannot
resign himself to the simple life of his friends who are now married;
pelota and fandango give him no pleasure and only evoke memories
of a happier past irretrievably lost. It is not surprising then that, when
his daring smuggler's plan to abduct Gracieuse from the convent
comes to nought and her resignation and faith show up even more

his own instability and anguish at their meeting there, Ramuntcho should finally leave the Basque country for South America. As the opening scene of the novel with its shrouds of rain enveloping Ramuntcho on a melancholy autumn evening denoted and as, later, his parting with his mother at the crossroads of the village and the outside world at sunset implied too, he has departed from his primitive Basque roots in Nature and faith forever and is now like "a plant uprooted from the soil of its Basque origins . . . which a flair for adventure has taken him away from"; while, as the spring blossoming of the flowers around the convent signify, Gracieuse has found in the traditions of her homeland the unique solution of life's problems recommended on every wayside crucifix in the Basque country—"Crux, ave, spes unica."

Ramuntcho is then "ein Gedicht einer Rasse[13]" in its epic depiction of Basque primitiveness and tradition threatened with extinction by the changes of the sophisticated modern world introduced from outside the region, as Loti was to point out in *L'Agonie de l'Euskalerria (Le Château de la Belle au Bois Dormant)*; and it was also a portrait of Loti himself at this time in its melancholy evocation of his nostalgia for his own lost simplicity and desire for faith, reflected in the heroine's bravery and the dragoon captain's conversion in his play on the persecution of his Huguenot ancestors on Oleron, *Judith Renaudin* (1898).[14]

Apart from when traveling to Paris or overseas and when he stayed at the now empty old house at Rochefort—his mother had died there on 12 November 1896—Loti lived for much of the rest of his life at Hendaye[15] and his impressions of the locality and his own existence there can be found in other volumes of his works besides *Ramuntcho.* The colorful pilgrimage of St. Martial, the Good Friday procession across the Spanish border at Irun, and the gradual erosion of Basque life by the advent of tourism are described in *Le Château de la Belle au Bois Dormant;* a Christmas Eve spent smuggling and a Sunday afternoon walk through Hendaye with a small boy are recalled in *Reflets sur la Sombre Route;* and the stalactite grotto of Isturitz, the sword dance of the *souletin* people of St. Jean de Luz, as well as Loti's visit in April, 1898, to Madrid to express his sympathy for Spain to the Queen Regent when America attacked Cuba and his stops en route at Burgos and Loyola are all depicted in *Figures et Choses qui passaient.*

VII   L'Inde (sans les Anglais)

On 15 April 1898 Loti was retired early from the navy as part of a government policy brought in by Edouard Lockroy to introduce young fresh blood into the higher ranks. Loti, like so many of his fellow officers, protested at this and thanks no doubt to Mme Adam's intervention was reinstated on 24 February 1899. For the next eighteen months or so Loti was placed in the service of the Ministry of Foreign Affairs and in November, 1899, set out for India to present a French decoration to the Maharajah of Travancore and to carry out certain other minor commissions. A travelogue of his journey is provided by his impressions in *L'Inde (sans les Anglais).*

As is suggested by the title[16] of the volume, first published in the July and September, 1902, and January and February, 1903, issues of the *Revue des Deux Mondes,* and its dedication to the Boer President Kruger, Loti's India comprises those aspects of India untouched by the colonialist and civilizing influences of Britain, whose expansion overseas he disliked as a French naval officer and of whose Westernizing he disapproved both as an exoticist and a seeker of simplicity and faith; Loti's India was then not to be that later described by E. M. Forster, but rather a select view of the continent that would reflect his own desire for vitality and simple faith and his thoughts on death. His route takes him by zebu cart from Kandy to Anuradhapura in Ceylon, by boat across the Gulf of Manar to Palancota, on by horse-drawn carriage to Trivandrum in Travancore, then by a large rowing boat through the lagoons of Cochin and on by road to Madurai, Trichinopoly, Pondichéry, Madras and Hyderabad, whence he takes the train to Udaipur, Jaipur, Agra, and Benares. As in his trek across Arabia to Jerusalem, Loti's tour of India also has a religious mission; when he enters the Red Sea on his way to Ceylon, he is still filled with dark thoughts about death and the void beneath the illusions of human existence, but the dazzling light of the sun by day and the calm of the starry sky at night encourage him to think that he might discover faith and peace in the Brahminism of ancient India; hence it is the unchanged and old India which he seeks and describes with his usual detailed impressionism.

It is an India of great contrasts, often existing side by side: The lush jungle with its crocodiles and elephants of Ceylon, the fertile plains of Travancore with their quiet village life, the palm groves and lagoons of Cochin, and the simple pastoral region of Madurai remind Loti of his homeland by their natural vegetation and the birds and insects which live in it; while the parched plateau of Hyderabad and the mountainous desert outside Jaipur with their sparse vegetation and scavenging rats, jackals, and birds of prey show quite a different aspect of India. A similar contrast is found in the people Loti describes; now he is with sophisticated princes with diamonds in their turbans who live in luxurious palaces amid beautiful gardens such as those at Trivandrum, Udaipur and Jaipur and have their own soldiers, elephants, and pet panthers, all of which are groomed with equal splendor or he is with beautiful princesses and singers; now with ascetic, dust-covered fakirs, long-haired Brahmins, clad in just a loincloth and with the monogram of Vishnu on their foreheads and the white cord of their initiation across their shoulder, and the starving thousands he compassionately gives money to on the train to Jaipur and is shocked to see dying in the streets of that rich city. This apparent contrast lies, however, at the very basis of Indian religious life, as Loti finds out when he visits the grottos of Ellora, where the red and green statues of Shiva and the black pebble or *linga* denote the juxtaposition of procreation and death in the Hindu creed, and at Benares, where the Ganges is used both by the living and the dead and is as creative and destructive at the same time in its flood as the harsh sun of the Hyderabad desert that both nurtures and starves its victims. Life and death, sensuality and asceticism, luxury and poverty are all part of the Hindu view of a good life and of human aspirations toward the world-soul and reincarnation.

Loti is not slow to appreciate the sensual beauty of the Indian people: He compares the virile grace of the bronzed, hirsute men and youths he sees to Greek statues and finds Indian women with their silk saris and golden bracelets quite bewitching when he meets the Maharani of Travencore and the actress Balamoni at Madurai and watches a sensuous dancer at the quaint French city of Pondichéry.

At the same time as his artistic eye is drawn to the colorful and sensual vitality of India, he is attracted by the strange asceticism and Buddhic pose of contemplative meditation of the fakirs and wants to gain insight into the Brahmin's cult of spiritual detachment. To do this he visits the mystics' mountain shrine of Trichinopoly with its tunneled places of worship, figure of Ganesa, and summit fire; he goes, too, to the huge Shri-Ragam temple there with its twenty-one red-granite pyramids covered with statues of gods with multiple arms and legs and watches the preparations for the annual procession of the sacred Vishnu image on a heavy wooden chariot decorated with red silk curtains, flowers, and naked youths, which he sees the next day being pulled along on ropes by hosts of men followed by a cortege of sacred elephants; he visits the temple at Madurai with its massive sculptured columns and sacred peacocks and elephants, sees its treasures, and watches from among the crowds, assembled on the lake's steps with their rushes and lamps, the annual trip of the embryo-like images of Shiva and his wife Parvati round the lake. He also consults two Brahmins at Udaipur about their faith, but they are too ascetic and detached from the world to help him; he seeks too the aid of the theosophers of Madras but is as unable to accept their Buddhist positivism as he is the childishly colorful idolatry of the Hindus; only at Benares after visiting the House of the Masters, where Annie Bezant instructs him in an esoteric Buddhism, does he feel a greater detachment and less fear of death as he watches the crowds on the Ganges praying to the world-soul to which they submit their individuality and burning their dead in the belief of ultimate reincarnation.

The fact, however, that Loti continued to give his personal, artistically refined impressions of his travels to the public shows that the loss of his individualism and detachment was but momentary; this is seen when he describes the beauty of a girl about to be cremated while admiring the detachment of the crowds praying. Furthermore, the fact that among his impressions of India those of his visits to the huge remains of palaces and cities of the vanished past of the Sinhalese and Jahan Moguls—Anuradhapura, Golconda, Gwalior, Agra, Amber—have quite a large place suggests that Loti was still as much nostalgically attracted to the past and filled with his own dread of death without faith, which he saw represented in these now abandoned, melancholy sites, as he was fascinated by the unspoilt exoticism of the motley street scenes in Hyderabad or the pink city of Jaipur and by the simple faith of the crowds at Benares. As at the end of *Jérusalem,* Loti might recommend faith and the Hindu *Vedas* to others like himself in *L'Inde (sans les Anglais),* but he himself was as much in need of faith and stability as before his visit.[17]

VIII   Vers Ispahan

In early April, 1900, Loti, accompanied by a French sailor, left Bombay for Persia which he had heard about from his neighbor at Hendaye, Mme Dieulafoy, an explorer. After a brief stop, described in *Le Château de la Belle au Bois Dormant,* at the humid, dazzling white port of Muscat where the young Iman presented his French visitor with a fine dagger and sword from his own collection, Loti reached Bender-Bouchir, the caravan terminus of the route from the Persian Gulf to the religious center of Isfahan. Here, the two men were forced to spend a week in quarantine before setting off on the night of 17 April with their *tcharvadar* or guide, Abbas, three armed soldiers, and a small train of recalcitrant mules loaded with provisions for the climb over the series of plateaux and mountains on their way to Shiraz, Isfahan, and Teheran. Loti recorded his experiences of this journey, often at night because of the heat in the daytime, and for a large part of the way either over stony and sandy desert studded with the occasional oasis and crumbling village or up steep mountainsides where ravines, landslides, and brigands were a constant danger, in his volume *Vers Ispahan,* published in the *Revue des Deux Mondes* from 15 December 1903 to 15 February 1904.

Despite all the varied difficulties and delays en route—loading the mules in a strong wind at night, crossing the mountains in the dark, finding and keeping relays of guides and horsemen to accompany them, and seeking out lodgings at the caravan stages and in the hamlets and towns, when they eventually found their way to them through the thick ramparts, winding alleyways and bazaars which characterize Persian and most Islamic communities—Loti enjoyed the pilgrimage. He liked riding along with wild Persian horsemen with long black moustaches and clad in flowing robes and tall astrakhan hats across miles of virginal desert perfumed by clumps of aromatic wild flowers where nomads with herds of sheep and cows still roamed: over rock formations unchanged since the Creation and inhabited only by birds of prey; and through oat and cornfields dotted with poppies, and valleys of trees and birds lying in between the high, snow-covered mountains. Cut off from the outside world by these high plateaux, Persia had not been exploited by the West as India had been; here, time had stood still just as it had for Loti in parts of Morocco and Arabia; Nature was still untouched and virginal; there were no railways nor factories to spoil the idyllic peace and beauty of the vast openness; here, one could still sit on hand-woven carpets under flowering orange trees, sip one's tea, smoke one's *kalyan*, and dream away the warm afternoon, as Loti and other travellers did at the quaint even if rather sordid village of Konoridjé; it was as if an old Persian print had come to life. As elsewhere, such naturalness stimulates Loti's romantic imagination: the unspoilt charm of Nature reminds Loti of Limoise, and the primitive villages and countryside he sees evoke ancient Gaul; while the horsemen that accompany him and the fierce black-bearded travelers he sees in the old fortress of Myan-Kotal recall for him the Assyrian profiles he read of in his childhood and later sees on the ruins of Persepolis; and the crenellated forts guarded by bearded warriors in long robes which they pass in the desert make him think of the Crusades; life seemed, as in Morocco, to have barely altered in Persia since the days of the poets Hafiz and Sa'di, whose tombs Loti visits in Shiraz, or of Shah Abbas who built the beautiful mosques of Isfahan.

As is implied by the fanaticism of the dervishes whom Loti watches sweating and bleeding in the frenzied chanting of their prayers at Koumichan and Makandbey and who threaten him at a café in Shiraz; by the silence and privacy of the narrow, dark streets of Shiraz, especially after sunset and the muezzin's final prayer; by the completely veiled figures of the women whom Loti sees darting like phantoms behind the high walls of their lodgings and whose faces he never manages to catch a glimpse of; and by the fact that Loti cannot find lodgings in the holy quarter of Isfahan and has to be accommodated in the Russian consulate next door and protected by Russian guards when he goes out, after the hovel he does find is besieged by an angry crowd, Islam still weighs heavily on Persian life and it is this that has preserved the country's unspoilt traditional culture. This is represented in Loti's account particularly by Persian architecture and furnishings: the turquoise blue and gold porcelain which cover with arabesques and motifs of flowers and fruit the domes of Isfahan's mosques and the Moorish architecture of its university, the interior of the vizir of Shiraz' palace with its old carpets, red velvet cushions, and the rose-patterned porcelain mosaic of its walls, the green and gold splendor of the tomb of Fatima and the spires, minarets, and blue domes of Nasr-ed-din's mosques

at Koum, and the precious porcelain and crystal collection of the
Shah at Teheran. The fact that Loti sees Isfahan when all the roses
are blooming and the city is decorated and perfumed by them brings
the past glory of Shah Abbas' Persia all the more romantically and
poetically alive, as Loti sits in a café there, rose in hand, having his
tea and *kalyan* and dreaming of the bearded horsemen of the
past in their brocade and kashmir robes riding fine, bejeweled
steeds along the *Tcharbag,* an avenue specially constructed by the
Shah with plane trees, roses, and fountains. Furthermore, the high
altitude and surrounding desert cause the air and light to be clearer
and more intense than elsewhere and the lapis lazuli shades of the
domes and walls create a sort of pseudoreligious, awe-inspiring
apotheosis of blues in Loti's eyes, particularly at night in the bril-
liant rays of the stars.

Isfahan's temporary excess of beauty of blue porcelain and roses
reflects Loti's momentary religious awe in this unspoilt center of
Islam; the despair of not attaining faith that follows is represented as
elsewhere by images of decay and death. Thus, according to Loti,
Persia's culture like Morocco's and Japan's is, despite the splendor
of the mosques and the profusion of roses, gradually dying. Pieces
of porcelain are cracking and falling away from the domes and walls,
buildings are crumbling, streets are full of filth and bodies of dead
animals litter the roofs of houses and the highways, awaiting the
vultures. The colossal dark gray blocks and twenty sleek monoliths
with their friezes of bearded hunters and gateways of huge winged
bulls of Persepolis, former capital of the Persia of Darius and
Xerxes and now mere isolated ruins overgrown with weeds, provide
a melancholy backcloth to Loti's impressions of the beautiful but
moribund Persia of today.

If such great empires like those whose ruins Loti saw in Palestine
and India could fall, then clearly the decline of Persia was also
part of the mysterious evolution of history which was transforming
countries like Japan and Morocco through contact with Western
civilization. Shiraz and Isfahan might still be cut off from the outside
world and its modern inventions, but Teheran, which was founded
more recently, already showed signs of foreign influence. Its buildings
were new, its roads were wider, and its royalty and vizirs had been
educated in the West and their residences furnished in European
style; the people here were less primitive and fanatical and some of

them, like Loti's driver and guides from Teheran to Enzeli and Batum on the Caspian Sea, were already falling prey to alcoholism, a scourge of European society. As elsewhere, the decline of simple life and traditional culture coincides with French and British expansion overseas. In nostalgically describing with his refined sensibility the moribund splendor of Persia's age-old culture and its natural simplicity in *Vers Ispahan,* Loti is, as a product of French civilization with its decadent oversophistication, deploring his own and France's consequent loss of the primitiveness and traditionalism related to faith that once created both Persepolis and Isfahan.

CHAPTER 7

The Return to a Disenchanted World

I Les Derniers Jours de Pékin

O N 3 August 1900, only a month after returning from India and
Persia, Loti was leaving Cherbourg on the "Redoutable" bound
for China, the country on which the attention of the Western world
had been focused ever since news of the recent Boxer rising had
reached Europe. Loti was to be aide-de-camp to Vice-Admiral
Pottier, who was in charge of the French naval forces sent to
China along with those of the other European powers to suppress
the rebellion and bring help to those Westerners who survived it.
On his arrival on 29 September in the Gulf of Pechili, Loti was sent
by Pottier to Peking to take certain papers to the French legation
in the city and to appraise the situation there now that the siege
of the European concessions was over. His impressions of his
journey by train from Taku, where he landed, to Tien-Tsin and Yang-
Sun and then on by junk along the Pei-Ho River as far as Tong-
Chu, whence he was driven to Peking, and his stay in the city in
October–November, 1900, and May, 1901,[1] were recorded first in
articles in *Le Figaro* and the *Revue Illustrée* in 1900 and then in
Les Derniers Jours de Pékin, published in February, 1902.

His journey to Peking takes him under a significantly cold
autumn sky past a gray, dusty landscape covered in unharvested
fields of rotting millet, burned-out ruins of houses, cemeteries,
dozens of corpses and refugees, and a motley assortment of British,
German, Austrian, French, Russian, Japanese, and American
troops camping in deserted, ruined hamlets. Everywhere he goes he
finds the cinders and scarred beams of what were once small wooden
houses; in Tong-Chu he wanders through the ruins of the city's
winding streets bespattered with the broken porcelain and other
bloodstained belongings of their former inhabitants; among the
silent ruins he comes across the bloodstained, dismembered, and
mutilated bodies of the Boxers' victims strewn over the ground
and discovers the head and legs of a woman in separate buckets

110

hidden in the ruins of what appears to have been a hotel; and he watches a mangy, starving dog eating at the leg of a dead child while crows circle overhead awaiting their turn.[2] The few people who remain, like the mother and daughter Loti finds, are either too petrified to move or flee with the little they still possess. Loti's description of an old Chinese woman fleeing her ruined home when German soldiers invade it and smash her few belongings and small altar is —like that of the forts of the Great Wall of China at Taku now being taken over by the international detachments of troops, each with their flag flying and anthem being played—symbolic of the fate of the great Manchu empire.

Death, destruction, and an autumnal melancholy at the passing of a great and mysterious empire continue to dominate Loti's impressions as he makes his way with Osman, his naval orderly, an armed soldier from Normandy named Renaud, and a Chinese boy, Tum, along the Pei-Ho, the banks of which are strewn with mutilated corpses and still reverberate with the gunfire of Japanese and German patrols and marauding Boxers. His arrival in the snow before the silent, massive walls of Peking after crossing miles of dry, dusty steppes from Tong-Chu, the gray rubble and burned houses he sees in the empty streets beyond the Tartar Gate, and the European flags he finds flying there only confirm these impressions; while the accounts he hears of the heroic defense of the French legation and Catholic concession against the Boxers and the piles of mutilated bodies he sees not only confirm Loti's impressions of Chinese cruelty, but evoke in him that same admiration of Christian heroism as he had for his Huguenot ancestors.

Above all, however, Loti's impressions of Peking are dominated by his feeling that the beauty and mystery of China's Imperial City have been destroyed by the Boxer rising and desecrated by the occupying troops. As he implies right at the beginning of his account, when the masts, guns, and flashing lights of the European fleets suddenly loom up out of the mysterious silence and emptiness of the Gulf of Pechili, the veil of China's inaccessibility and secrecy has been rent and the sacred and hitherto inaccessible parts of the Imperial City, now devoid of its sublime and virtually invisible Son of Heaven and his family, have been exposed to the world after centuries of strict seclusion behind a whole series of high walls and moats. When Loti visits the Temple of Heaven, he finds the woods and avenues surrounding it occupied by British troops from India, who are using the temple's incense burner for incinerating the diseased corpses of cattle, and discovers that the lacquered scarlet and gold circular sanctuary has been pillaged. He watches soldiers—not French ones, of course, who are depicted as the Chinaman's friend—breaking up the puppets of the Imperial theater, smashing porcelain, ivory, and silk robes once belonging to the Empress which were stored in a Gothic church in the Imperial City, and sees the vandalism done by soldiers in the apartments of the Empress's palace in the Lotus Lake. Furthermore, the Marble Bridge is strewn with corpses, the drained Lotus Lake is like a stagnant marsh, and there is a great breach in the walls of the North Palace.

However, deplorable as the situation may be, it does give Loti an opportunity to enter the hidden world of the Chinese Emperors as well as to pillage the Empress's tiny slippers and a throne, which he used at a Chinese-style party he was later to give at Rochefort, and to dress up in princely robes and smoke opium in the Imperial City. From 20 October to 3 November he is accommodated with other officers in the sumptuous North Palace with its galleries of mirrors, cloisonné screens, ebony tables, gold figures of animals and monsters, yellow carpets patterned with dragons, ivory, and porcelain; he visits the Palace of the Ancients, where he sees Primitive-like paintings of the Chinese court through the ages on ebony scrolls hidden away for centuries in lacquered cupboards and the tomb, jade statue, and seals of Emperor Kuang-Su; he follows the straight avenue bordered with huge marble figures of monsters and howling dogs which leads majestically through a series of high red walls and gateways to the marble galleries and courtyards at the end of which—at the very axis of Peking's four cities—lie three identical throne rooms where the Emperor would appear beside a red and gold throne enclosed by walls and ceilings patterned with dragons; he goes through the Empress's apartments with their gold ceilings, mirrors, ebony carvings, animal figures in bronze and gold, artificial flowers in agate, amber and jade, private oratory, and miniature gardens; and he later, on a second journey to Peking, makes a visit to the tombs of four of the Emperors hidden out in the country by huge red ramparts and thick forest.

The former magnificence of Peking is, however, gone forever: Everywhere there is silence; everywhere, from the ancient temple of the lamas he visits to the avenues and courtyards leading to the Imperial throne, the colors of the walls are fading and the white of the marble is going yellow just as in the streets of Peking the gold monster figures on the eaves of houses are discolored by the dust and the weather; and grass is beginning to grow over the paving stones of the palaces and avenues. Peking is as effete as the decadent Imperial occupant of the dark bedroom with its blue-black curtains and refined perfume of tea and pressed roses, which Loti is shown into, and the sickly, opium-smoking prince clad in precious silks and heavily perfumed with musk, whom he meets on his way to the Emperor's tombs. Except in the primitive communities in the country where Loti is ceremoniously welcomed by local mandarins and entertained by village stilt-dancers, jugglers, and gymnasts on his way to the tombs, the strict tradition-alism and isolationism of Chinese life as epitomized in the Imperial City is being undermined by its Western invaders owing to its decadent condition. Railways are to be constructed from Hanchow right up to the Imperial City; and, as is shown by the funeral beside the Lotus Lake of a German general killed in a fire in one of the palaces—for which Loti makes his second visit to Peking—the ball arranged by General Marchand in the Imperial City, and the avenue named after General Voyron, Peking has been surrendered to the West; and with it, all the mystery and charm of one of the oldest and most unknown and unspoilt civilizations in history.

II   La Troisième Jeunesse de Madame Prune

In between Loti's two visits to Peking and after his expedition to the tombs of the Emperors and a further stay in the Gulf of Pechili, the "Redoutable" took him, partly because of Admiral Pottier's and the crew's deteriorating health in the torrid heat of the Yellow Sea and their need for relaxation, to Japan and also, for a few days, to Korea. If the exposure of the Imperial City to the Western world had put an end to one of the exotic mysteries which had excited Loti's imagination in childhood and shown him once more that the world of the past was rapidly changing, then his return to the land of Madame Chrysanthème after fifteen years was similarly to impress on Loti that times were changing and the past and his youth were gone forever. An account of his stay in

Nagasaki from December, 1900, to the following April and again
in July and October, 1901, his stop at Seoul, the ship's call at
Yokohama, and its route through the Inland Sea back to Nagasaki
is given in *La Troisième Jeunesse de Madame Prune,* which Loti
wrote largely at Istanbul[3] in 1904 and which was first published,
dedicated to the crew of the "Redoutable," in the *Revue des Deux
Mondes* from 15 December 1904 to 1 February 1905.

After arriving in heavy seas and a snowstorm in the steep corridor
of Nagasaki harbor, Loti soon gets used to seeing Japan in the
cold and snow; he becomes accustomed once more to the small
wooden houses, the old pagodas with their granite monster figures,
the cemeteries on the mountainside, and the waterfalls, trees, ferns,
and mosses which cover it; and to the slit-eyed, smiling, bowing
mousmés, bowler-hatted men, seminaked rickshawmen, and the
polite and affected hostesses of the teahouses. He discovers that
Madam Chrysanthème is now married to a lanternmaker; he meets
Madame Prune, widowed and as charming and astute as ever in her
propositions for his future romance; he returns to the Teahouse
of the Cranes and becomes friendly with Mlle Pluie d'Avril, who
dances for him in her flowing kimono patterned with gold
chrysanthemums and monstrous masks and attracts him by her
slim, feline figure and cat's eyes; he sees again Madame Ours who
sells flowers on the way to the cemetery and becomes acquainted
with Madame Ichihara and Mlle Matsumoto who sell monkeys;
and he meets Mlle Inamoto, the young, charming daughter of a
temple priest, in the fields by the cemetery each day and has a
nascent and somewhat enigmatic affection for her since she is less
affected and more natural than most Japanese girls he comes
across. Loti thus rediscovers to some extent the life he led at
Dioudjendji. He accompanies Madame Prune to place flowers on
the tomb of her husband, M. Sucre; he visits the bare, humble
home of Mlle Pluie d'Avril; he goes to the theater and finds himself among an audience of women who have come complete with
their pipes and babies to watch a comedy about cuckoldry; he
visits the temples of the Fox and of the Horse of Jade with their
old granite steps and columns and once gilded cedarwood exterior;
and enjoys walking amid the peace and naturalness of the mountainside forests.

As fifteen years earlier, he is puzzled by the apparent contradiction which he sees in the Japanese character and that is epitomized in the contrast between the politeness and delicacy of the teahouse and geisha culture and the gruesome monsters in granite or ivory he sees in temples and for sale on stalls and the masks and armor once used in war which he finds in souvenir shops. While he now accepts the affectation and superficiality of the Japanese, which had astonished and amused him before, he is this time much more aware of the gulf between the Oriental and Western view of life after the atrocities of the Boxers, and fears the strange gruesomeness underlying the Japanese character.

For Japan has become much more Westernized since his last stay here; the primitive junks of Nagasaki harbor are gone along with the moss-covered rocks by the waterfront and have been replaced by barges, steamers, and warships and a railway that feeds coal into a huge arsenal; the shops of the city are more Westernized in their window displays and an American advertisement for a food product mars the mountain peak; modern factories and other buildings have sprung up in the European quarter; and the Western scourge of drunkenness is now a frequent occurrence in the city. So Westernized has much of Japan become that Loti will at first not leave the "Redoutable" at Yokohama to witness its mass of electric wires, its arsenal, its factories, and shops crammed with shoddy pseudo-Japanese art; and when he does, however, land on the quay, he is shocked to be confronted with a Japanese journalist in frock coat and top hat who begins to interview him in English! The accounts he hears from his sailor friends who visit Tokyo and see the Empress now dressed in Parisian fashions and a students' antiforeigner demonstration make Loti regret the passing of old Japan and fear Japanese xenophobia even more. A quarrel he witnesses between French sailors and some fierce shopkeepers in Nagasaki, the disdain shown to him as a foreigner when some noblewomen visit the Teahouse of the Cranes, and the ferocious expression he glimpses on Mlle Pluie d'Avril's face only confirm Loti's suspicions that the same skill which is applied to making delicate bibelots and fitting Madame Prune's ebony-colored teeth with gold fillings may well be used soon for the purpose of war, which the Western powers have prompted by their interference in the Orient. Mlle Pluie d'Avril's Samurai dress in the geisha pageant anticipates this as does her inspecting the cannons when she is invited on board the "Redoutable." The idyllic Japanese culture and Nature-worship of the sacred island of Miyashima, which Loti visits on his course through the Inland Sea, and the unspoilt life of the primitive fishing villages on the Sea's shore will soon be eroded and the muscles and industry of the bronzed, hardy Japanese peasants will be employed in the forthcoming war with Russia, for which the Mikado is already imposing heavy taxes and the young people Loti sees are training.

As in Korea, where the decline of the aged Emperor and assassination of the Empress, the hatred of Westerners seen in the young heir to the throne and the desire for the benefits of European industrialization and warfare will soon bring about the extinction of Korean culture with its strange costumes and dances, so in Japan, too, simple natural beauty and the ancient culture it has inspired will be destroyed and only the horrible and ugly aspects of the Japanese character will remain to promote war. This transformation is expressed not only in the news of Madame Chrysanthème's pregnancy and Madame Prune's suffering from the "change of life," but also in Loti's farewell to the charming, simple Inamoto, who symbolizes Japan's vanished past in contrast to the other two women who represent its decadence, near the abandoned, decaying temple and tombs of Nagasaki ablaze in the glow of the autumnal sunset; as the first New Year of the century and the gunfire announcing Queen Victoria's death signify to Loti, the age of his childhood simplicity is over for good; time has passed even if the dwarf trees of Madame Prune's miniature garden have barely grown and recall his earlier visit here. His discovery of the proximity of the Teahouse of the Cranes to the crematorium implies that death alone now awaits both Loti and old Japan.

III   Un Pélerin d'Angkor

Another stop on Loti's voyage home from China was, however, to remind him further that his youth was gone and his life spent and convince him of the passing of all things—his visit to Angkor Wat. On 19 November 1901, the "Redoutable" arrived at Saigon, where it was to stay until 8 December, and Loti arranged with the help of the colonial governor Paul Doumer to go with his servant, a Chinese boy, and an interpreter to explore the famous ruins of the twelfth-century city of the Khmer empire discovered in the heart of the Cambodian jungle. As Loti explains at the beginning of *Un Pèlerin d'Angkor,* the volume he published on his expedition in 1912, this ruined city lost in the heart of the jungle had fascinated him ever since he had seen a picture of it in a magazine while going through his brother's papers in his "museum" at Rochefort one April evening during his childhood; for him, Angkor became at once the ultimate goal of his exotic dreams of those early years, a last hope against the vanity and passing of all things, of which the family Bible reading, that then interrupted his musings on the lost city, already warned him. Loti's expedition forty years or more later thus not only fulfills a childhood ambition, but also represents the last possible solace of his exoticism against the anguish of a life deprived of the simple faith of his youth and now approaching its end like the world of the past around him.

From Saigon Loti takes the train on 25 November 1901 through a flat landscape of ricefields to Mytho, where he embarks on a small sampan which takes him along the flooded banks of the Mekong River to the old, silent capital of Pnom-Penh and then up almost to Siem Reap. Here he leaves behind the tropical river bank with its groves of coconut palms, bananas, mangroves and bamboo, its primitive fishing villages on stilts, its flocks of pelicans, egrets, and marabous and numbers of monkeys and reptiles clinging to the lianas and trees dipping in the oily, feverish, insect-infested water and takes to a mandoline-shaped bullock-cart for the two-hour journey through the cooler, highly scented forest to Angkor. When he at last catches sight of the gray, tiara-shaped towers of Angkor's temples in a vast clearing in the jungle, he is really too tired and hot to appreciate them, and the light of the midday sun is too bright to show them up to advantage; already, he feels a certain disillusionment. When he visits the temples next morning, after a cursory visit the previous evening which is cut short by the swooping of swarms of bats hanging on the ruins, he wanders through the long, low galleries which encircle the pyramid-shaped towers at three levels and are joined by increasingly steeper steps to the sanctuary at the top; these cloister-like galleries, reminiscent of a cavern in their dampness and in the greenish light that penetrates from their small windows, are covered in bas-reliefs depicting barebreasted Hindu *apsaras* posing in their dances, seven-headed cobras, lions, and scenes from the *Ramayana* showing battles between demons and gods. Unfortunately, the original paint and gold has been worn away by the damp and by pilgrims touching it and now appears black and defaced by spiders' webs and excrement from the bats; as Loti climbs to the third circle of galleries, some ninety feet above the ground, it begins to rain and he takes refuge in this last cloister before the seemingly inaccessible sanctuary, only to find even more crumbling ruins than on the lower levels and a motley collection of statues of Buddha mutilated by time and deformed by layers of bat excrement; and when he does reach the sanctuary, he finds it bare and the giant Buddha which stands in it still placidly smiling beneath a coating similar to that disfiguring the statues below.

Loti also visits the nearby ruins of the city of Angkor-Tom and sanctuary of Bayon built some four hundred years before the temples at Angkor Wat; here, the ruins of some fifty towers with figures of mythological monsters, three-headed elephants, and strange smiling faces on them are strewn beneath the cavernous greenery of the forest which is gradually strangling them with its creepers and lianas just as the rain and steamy dampness is corroding Angkor Wat; where there was once a city of a million people decorated with a strange and magnificent architecture of towers crowned with a giant golden lotus, there is now only silence, jungle, and rubble; Nature is reclaiming possession of this remote site which once witnessed the rise of the mysterious Khmer empire and now reflects its equally mysterious disappearance. Only the dancing of the young girls dressed in gold and pagoda-shaped headgear, which the moribund King Norodon arranges for Loti in his equally decaying capital, brings alive perhaps for the last time the scenes and faces depicted on the ruins as part of Cambodia's sacred and mysterious Khmer heritage; for France has already begun to exploit and spoil this latest of her colonies by bringing these dancers to Europe and revealing their strange culture to the world

For Loti the decline of Angkor symbolizes his own; his disillusionment at its ruined state puts an end to the mystery and excitement of his childhood dreams of the exotic; whereas forty years earlier he had all of life before him and, stimulated by the objects in his "museum," he looked forward to the strange and exotic, which Angkor epitomized, now his life is virtually over and he has had his fill of travel and adventure. The source of his exoticism, his "museum," has remained the same and so has the view from it over Rochefort, but Loti himself is no longer a child and he has no longer the hope and faith he had then; now, as he looks again at the dusty picture of Angkor of years ago, he is reminded of the biblical warning of Ecclesiastes on the passing of all things including human desires and aspirations and can only hope after his visits to so many holy places all over the world that the God of Pity, to whom they are almost unanimously devoted, exists as a solace for the harshness of an otherwise vain reality.

IV   Les Désenchantées

Loti arrived back in France after his tour of duty in the Far East on 14 March 1902; he was to stay at Rochefort for most of the following eighteen months, first on three months' convalescence and leave and then serving as an aide to the Maritime Prefect of the port from 23 October 1902 to 10 September 1903. During this time he wrote his accounts of his travels in India, Persia, China, and Japan; he collaborated with his friend Emile Vedel in a translation of *King Lear,* which Antoine produced at the Odéon with great success on 30 November 1904; and he saw to the construction in the old house at Rochefort of the mosque and Chinese room from material he had bought for fifteen thousand francs from a demolished mosque at Damascus, and objects he had pillaged in China; here, too, he preserved his mother's room exactly as it was on the day she died and kept in the mosque a replica of the original tombstone of Hakidjé, believing it to be visited by her spirit.[4] When he was not living amid the sentimental, pseudo-exotic atmosphere of Rochefort, he would retire to his retreat at Hendaye, witnessing the gradual passing of the traditional life of the Basques as more and more tourists flowed into the region. Despite several parties, such as the Chinese one in May, 1903, and the occasional visitors—foremost among whom were Queen Natalie of Serbia for whom Loti had given a great banquet in October, 1899, and Mme Adam, with whom he could be almost as carefree and childish as he had been with his mother and sister[5]—Loti's life was now essentially a melancholy one; he was filled with a sense of the vanity and futility of his travels and pilgrimages; he had regained neither youthful simplicity nor faith and now that he was exhausted by the labors of his quest he could only brood on the imminence of death.

This, then, was Loti's mood when he was made naval attaché to the French Ambassador in Istanbul, M. Constans, and put in command for eighteen months of the cruiser "Vautour" and its attendant ship, the "Mouette," from 9 October 1903 to 24 March 1905.[6] The "Vautour," with its seven officers and 150 crew, was stationed at Istanbul and cruised off Greece and into the Adriatic from time to time as part of its program to promote French prestige in the Levantine area. Back in the land of Aziyadé, which he had made so famous and where he was so highly respected, Loti led as quiet a life as he could and tried to remain as incognito as possible; he therefore tried to avoid the European population, despite the entertaining he was obliged to do on board and his friend the Countess Ostrorog's introduction of him into high society, and enjoyed going in his turquoise caïque along the Bosphorus from Beïcos Bay opposite Therapia and Fondoukli near Pera, where his ship was docked, and wandering, wearing his fez, in the old Turkish parts of the city he knew so well.[7] During his stay he called on the Sultan and again visited Aziyadé's tomb and seeing it in a dilapidated condition decided, despite the difficulties to be overcome with regard to the Moslem authorities, to provide a new headstone for it.

As if after his travels his vain nostalgia for the past and his return to Istanbul had not made him sufficiently melancholy and aware of the changes in himself and the world since he had first come here, his contact and correspondence with three apparently Turkish women named Leyla, Neyr and Zeyneb, who wanted him to write a novel pleading the cause of the women in Turkish harems, was to draw his attention to a new development in his beloved Turkey. The three women, who wanted to exploit Loti's fame and sympathy for Turkey in this way, were in fact a French journalist specializing in the problem of women's rights, Mme Léra, known under the literary pseudonym of Marc Hélys, and two Turkish sisters she was related to, Zennour and Nouryé Noury-Bey, granddaughters of the Comte de Châteauneuf, who had become a Moslem and whose son had married a Circassian girl. Between them they thus had a more than adequate knowledge of life in a Turkish harem and of French to convince Loti of their authenticity; and the secrecy and risks involved in his meetings with them only made the venture all the more mysterious and exciting to him in his melancholy ennui. Zennour had written to Loti at Rochefort two years earlier, thanking him for writing *Aziyadé;* his first meeting with his three veiled correspondents was, however, with an officer from the "Vautour," Masméjean, at Tchiboukli on the Bosphorus on Saturday, 16 April 1904; other meetings took place on 26 April at the cemetery in Eyub, on 30 April at Feruz-Pacha mosque, on 26 November at a hospital in Taxim where Loti was recovering from influenza, on 12 December at the Belgian Legation, and on 14 December on board the "Vautour." All Loti's other meetings with the women were only with the two sisters; Marc Hélys returned to Paris and also went on to Sweden later, telling Loti that she had left for the Bosphorus and then Smyrna to be remarried. On 19 January 1905 Loti visited the sisters' house, which they had rearranged to look as Oriental as possible for his benefit, and on 19 February they went to see Aziyadé's new tombstone. At these meetings and in their correspondence, the three confided to Loti exaggerated versions of their own and others' harem experiences and Loti was satisfied with having so much exciting "inside" information on which to base his novel.

On his return to France in April, 1905, Loti began his novel, quoting in it most of the letters he had received from his three friends and just two of his own to them and describing their various meetings in Istanbul from his diary records as part of his presentation of their cause.[8] Leyla, Neyr, and Zeyneb—as Marc Hélys and the Noury sisters called themselves in their relations with Loti—become Djénane, Mélik, and Zeyneb in the novel; Loti himself is called André (originally Jean) Lhéry, his officer friend Masméjean is named Jean Renaud, and Aziyadé is referred to as Nedjibé; and the date and place of their meetings are altered slightly so as to preserve the mystery of the venture and prevent any unpleasant consequences for the women involved or Loti himself. The novel was thus fairly faithful to what actually took place and to what Loti was told about harem life, even though he invented an imaginary background and early life for Djénane built up on details received from his three friends, Mélek's premature death, and parts of Djénane's confession and her raising of her veil to emphasize certain aspects of his work's import. Entitled *Les Désenchantées,* the novel appeared, dedicated to Leyla (alias Marc Hélys) who, Loti had been informed, had committed suicide rather than remarry her former master, in the March to May, 1906, issues of the *Revue des Deux Mondes.*

From the very opening of the novel when the famous writer André Lhéry wearily reads among his correspondence a letter from his beloved Turkey in the melancholy solitude of his retreat in the increasingly modernized Basque country and his blond Circassian correspondent is seen awakening like a modern Sleeping Beauty in her luxurious chamber in her grandmother's house at Khassim-Pacha to face another empty day reading contemporary European writers, the fate of both are interwoven; for both of them are *désenchantés,* disillusioned by life, now that they have lost the simplicity and idealism of their youth. This is why Loti was so receptive to his three correspondents, whose outlook was so similar to his own, even though it was derived from quite different experiences, and why he wrote a novel apparently centered on a topic so alien to his respect for Islam; he could exploit the women's position and evidence to evoke his own mood now in Istanbul.

As is revealed by extracts from her letters to André and the diary she has kept since taking the veil, Zahidé, or Djénane—as she is later called—is disenchanted with life as a young Turkish girl traditionally destined to the harem of a husband imposed on her by her family; for such a course deprives her of the free enjoyment of all aspects of life shown her in her reading of modern European literature including Lhéry, which has been part of her Westernized education by a French governess.[9] Whereas she once submitted to Islamic tradition and the charm of its customs and beliefs when she was, like Aziyadé, a simple girl living in an idyllic Circassian village, now she has been initiated into Western ideas—particularly on freedom in love and skepticism in faith—and become used to Parisian clothes and furnishings and rebels against her fate; the spell cast by tradition on this Sleeping Beauty of Turkey has been broken by insight into a new and more exciting reality imported from the West; this twenty-two-year-old reader of Baudelaire and Nietzsche, who plays Wagner and César Franck and converses with her cousins in French, German, Italian and English, only obeys with reluctance the strict orders of her old-fashioned, simple-minded grandmother and resents the traditional restrictions of Islamic practice which requires bars on her windows, insists that she goes out veiled and escorted by a eunuch, and forbids her to be out after dusk. It is not surprising then that the marriage imposed on her to the Sultan's aide, young Captain Hamdi-bey, should make her even more rebellious and cause her much suffering; for she cannot love someone she will not even meet before her wedding and will only see a few times after it before becoming a mere instrument for his pleasure and lust and then being abandoned among the other inmates of his harem; yet she must go through with the wedding for there is little she can do to protest and she must smile when she thanks her father publicly for finding her such a fine husband, puts on the marriage crown, is led by the groom to be introduced to all the dozens of other women assembled in the harem, and is later courted by her husband prior to his possession of her body. When, after several years of merely satisfying Hamdi-bey's moments of desire, she returns from a period of convalescence to discover him embracing a young cousin who shortly afterward becomes pregnant, she seeks a divorce from him in a highly elaborate interview with the Sultan's wife; this is granted her somewhat melodramatically when the Sultan himself enters during the interview and feels compassion for her as she faints at his feet, overcome with her suffering and fear; and so she returns to Khassim-Pacha to join her cousins Mélek, who has also just gained a divorce after a great deal of suffering, and Zeyneb, whom her aged husband's death has released from bondage. For all three of them love has remained an unfulfilled dream; marriage has merely tainted their bodies and spoilt their health; their souls and minds, nurtured by sophisticated Western ideas and culture to expect so much, have been neglected and disillusioned by the simple traditional practices of old Turkey.

It is at this point, after their suffering in the harems, that André Lhéry, now much older than when he wrote *Nedjibé,* returns to Istanbul in 1904 to take up a post for two years, and after visiting Nedjibé's dilapidated tomb, which he decides to replace, receives a letter from the three women inviting him to meet them. Inspired by the memory of Nedjibé and encouraged by his friend Jean Renaud, he meets his correspondents first at Tchiboukli in a deserted café by the Bosphorus, then in the old cemetery at Eyub, in their faded Oriental-style home at Toussum-Ahga, in their nurse's crumbling old house near Sultan Selim mosque, in a harem near Mehmed-Fatih, and on visits to Nedjibé's tomb, Beïcos on the Bosphorus, and to the Eaux Douces. Like Loti, André Lhéry is excited by the whole venture—the risks involved in entering their meeting places and in meeting in the open and the mystery of his veiled friends—and cannot resist taking up the cause of the plight of Turkish women; for their suffering and disillusionment resemble his own at the loss of his simple youth and the past in a changing world. He realizes, however, at the tomb of Nebjidé, when he watches his three friends chanting the last rites there on his behalf and shortly afterward sees the snow falling on it, that his past, including his romance with her, is now truly dead; fascinated as he is by the Oriental dancing and character of his friends, which remind him of Nedjibé, he finally sees that their sophistication as well as his own age prevent him from engaging in such a simple romance again; and charmed as he is by the slow pace, contemplative tranquillity and proud traditionalism of the old quarters of the city with their mosques, cafés, and alleyways inhabited by turbaned imans and dervishes, he soon notices that people are already wearing European clothes and taking to alcohol, and factories and arsenals are gradually springing up here too; both he and Turkey have grown old and are leaving the past behind them; both are now *désenchantés* with the present reality just as are Djénane, Mélek, and Zeyneb.

Death awaits them all in the passing of time and the changes this brings about; both Mélek and Djénane die as victims of their modern education—the first from a fever contracted as a result of the suffering she bore in her unfortunate marriage and the threat of remarriage, and the second from poison taken in order to avoid being remarried to Hamdi-bey; André realizes, as he carries Mélek's coffin at her funeral and later when he sees Djénane lift her veil for the last time as a farewell to him at the moment his ship leaves, that the Turkey of his youth, where he found so much love, is fast approaching its end in the changes in its traditions brought about by time; and like Turkey, André knows his days of romance are over and he is near death, as he visits the deserted Eaux Douces for the last time in the November sunset. *Les Désenchantées* is then a self-confession expressed through the melancholy inspired by the Istanbul scene Loti sentimentally describes as well as being a somewhat melodramatic plea on behalf of young Turkish women contrived by the romantic imagination which Marc Hélys and her friends[10] shared with Loti himself.

V   La Mort de Philae

Loti returned home from Turkey on the "Phrygie" in early April, 1905, and spent the next six months convalescing; although he was only 55 years old, his active life and his writing up of his accounts of his travels at this time as well as his depressed state of mind were slowly exhausting him and taking their toll on his health. On 1 November 1905 he was put in command of the Fourth Maritime Depot at Rochefort until 13 September 1906, and on 2 August 1906 was given the rank of captain. In 1907 he accepted the invitation of the Khedive Abbas Hilmi to visit Egypt; here, he was to spend four months from January until mid-May touring the country, accompanied by his friend Mustapha Kemel; his impressions of the visit, somewhat biased by the nationalistic tendencies of his friend, are found in *La Mort de Philae*, which he completed in early November, 1908, and published in 1909.

As is implied by the title of the volume (originally proposed by Lord Redesdale) and by the opening description of the mysterious, awesome Sphinx smiling cynically in the pink moonlight of the silent desert and being wreathed toward dawn in a damp mist like an Apocalyptic vision because of the alteration in the Nile's course made by the British, Loti's impressions of Egypt are colored by his sense of the vanity of Man's efforts and his mortality in a world becoming more and more Westernized and materialistic. For Loti discovers on visiting Abydos, Thebes and Luxor that, whereas the colossal figures confidently holding the buckled cross of eternal life at the entrance to the temples of Amen and Osiris and their hypostyle's enormous columns and mural frescoes of jackal, falcon, and ibis-headed gods annotated with colorful hieroglyphics were once symbols of Ancient Egypt's and Man's early attempts at inmortal greatness and aspirations toward the eternal and unknowable, they are now, as they stand like fossils among dust and rubble crumbling in the constant heat and are desecrated by

Western tourists, an ironic reminder of Man's fragility and the apparent lack of eternal life for humanity. No trumpets have sounded in the four thousand years of Egypt's history to awaken the wrapped bodies of Amenophis, Seti, Ramses, or Queen Makeri to life everlasting; they remain as silent and still as the Sphinx, the Pyramids, and the avenue of rams, the lioness-headed goddesses and the statue of Sekhet, the ogress at Luxor, when Loti sees them in the Cairo Museum of Antiquities on a visit he makes there at night.

Furthermore, despite all the efforts of the Pharaohs to conceal and preserve their bodies after death for union with the Sun of the Dead Osiris and a semiconscious afterlife within their mummies by wrapping them in bandages, surrounding them with food and other requisites for their resurrection, and hiding them in huge granite tombs within secret underground passages covered in mythological murals such as those in the six-mile desert necropolis of Memphis and the rock tombs of the Valley of the Kings, their burial chambers had been increasingly despoiled through the ages and were now exposed to Western eyes; just as Cooks tourists here for their health or their pleasure desecrate Seti's temple to Osiris at Abydos by lunching in the grandiose ruins of its frescoed sanctuary and spoil the magnificence of the remains at Luxor with their hotels, so they swarm into the Cairo museum or the burial chambers at Thebes to see exposed and unswathed in the glare of electric lights the withered but recognizable features of the mighty rulers of the ancient world of four or five thousand years ago brought from their secret, silent tombs for their benefit. It was partly because Loti was so conscious of such profanation and disapproved of it that he visited many of the ruins and tombs at night or after the tourists had left; he could then appreciate in peace the mysterious and morbid fascination of these remote relics of the Ancients' desire for the Eternal and indulge his aesthetic sensibility in the nuances of shadows cast by the moonlight or sunshine on their titanesque statues and temples: shadows which emphasized their frozen muteness in the nocturnal silence of what were once great and famous centers of life and historical sites and reflected the comparatively ephemeral fragility of Man's efforts in contrast to the virtually eternal forces of Nature.

For Loti, the titanesque simplicity and vigorous idealism of this early civilization was now being prostituted to and desecrated by the largely skeptical representatives of a sophisticated, dilettantist

Western world in the natural evolution of history just as idyllic modern Egypt was being slowly Westernized by British colonialism and Cooks tourism; the historic Nile was being tamed with the dam at Aswan and the alteration of its course near Cairo to provide for greater cotton cultivation; its primitive water-drawers or *shadûfs* and all the other bronzed, handsome villagers who lived by its banks were being replaced by steam-operated waterworks just as their cornfields were giving way to factories and their *dahabiyas* to dynamo-driven launches; instead of carrying the processions of the Pharaohs and their ancient gods, the Nile now conveyed launches, named after the mighty rulers of the past but full of Cooks tourists, and transported sugar or cotton crops on their way to British factories. And just as the old quarters and quiet mosques of Cairo were crumbling and the new city was fast becoming Westernized with its electric lights, hotels, inns and brothels, so too was that ancient city on the Nile, Aswan, now being turned into a neo-European spa with gardens, hotels, souvenir stalls, excursions by donkey or hackney carriage, and trips by dynamo-powered launches up the river, and corrupted by drink and prostitution.

The last chapter in Loti's account of his stay in Egypt on his excursion to the Isle of Philae, once the sanctuary of Isis, epitomizes the modern fate of Egypt; the British have half submerged the temple by raising the level of the Nile to provide more irrigation for their cotton cultivation; what was once a sacred place is being defaced and crumbling under the influence of the water flooding its interior; only the tops of the columns lining the sacred avenue leading to the sanctuary are now visible; and its age-old peacefulness and sanctity is being interrupted by the arrival of noisy tourists in boats carrying the British flag and the echoes of the "hip, hip, hurrah!" exclaimed by the Arab boatmen in these holy precincts to please their modern clients; while the nearest village to this ancient temple, connected by rail, steamer and telegraph to Aswan, is filled with workers from the nearby factories indulging in the drink, prostitution, and pornography imported there from the West. The faithless materialism and decadent sophistication of Europe epitomized in the colonialism and tourism of the British are thus not only profaning the mysterious sanctity of Ancient Egypt's spiritual heritage, but also undermining the Islamic way of life of modern Egypt.

Loti's account of his stay in Egypt reflected once again, as had his visits to the Far East and Turkey and, to a lesser extent, his pilgrimages earlier to the Middle East, Persia and India, his spiritual despair at the irretrievable loss of the simplicity and faith he longed for and of the emotional security of his childhood; this mood of despair and disillusionment was in turn poetically evoked in his impressions of the world of the past coming to an end. All that was simple and idyllic and traditional was being corrupted and spoilt by the materialistic sophistication of Europe's industrial powers trying to progress and establish themselves overseas; all that was sacred, mysterious or exotic was being exposed and undermined by the soulless skepticism and conformism of Europe—symbolized in Westernization and tourism—which sought it in their quest for new values but only to destroy or prostitute it soon after. The death of Philae refers to the decline of all these elements in the evolving modern world in which Loti saw himself like the legendary Sleeping Beauty who gave her name in 1910 to his volume of essays *Le Château de la Belle au Bois Dormant* largely concerned with the passing of the natural and traditional around Saintonge and the Basque country; he was waking up in middle age and finding that all the elements mentioned above, which he had cherished from his childhood, now appeared to be declining too. In Loti's thought, only death seemed to lie before him and all he liked and longed for;[11] in reality, his views were overpessimistic and exaggerated on account of the selection and distortion of impressions he made in order to evoke the mood of utter despair at his own Western sophistication and skepticism. It was in the soul and mind of Loti rather than in the world of the new century that death loomed so large.

CHAPTER 8

A Voice in Europe's Wilderness

I *The End of Loti's Naval Career*

ON 1 August 1907, shortly after his stay in Egypt, Loti was granted *résidence conditionnelle,* a state of semiretirement which allowed him time to concentrate on his literary pursuits, attend the *première* of his play *Ramuntcho* at the Odéon in February, 1908, and speak at the presentation of his friend Jean Aicard at the Académie in December, 1909, as well as to recover from the fatigue of his travels and writing. Apart from these engagements and a short visit to London from 5 to 11 July 1909, when his antipathy for the British was mellowed by his audience with Queen Alexandra at Buckingham Palace on 10 July and he was pleasantly surprised to discover that the British people were more hospitable and the capital more full of trees and flowers than he had imagined,[1] Loti spent these last years as a naval captain at home in Rochefort and Hendaye. On 14 January 1910 Loti retired from the navy after 42 years, 3 months and 13 days service, of which 19 years, 11 months and 8 days had been at sea;[2] from being a mere *aspirant,* he had climbed his way up to the rank of ship's captain; his only regret was that he had never reached that of admiral.

II   Suprêmes Visions d'Orient, 1910

Although the days of his naval voyages were now officially over, one place still fascinated Loti and called him back: Turkey. On 15 August 1910 he arrived at Istanbul, where he was to spend the next two months. An account of his stay, some of it taken directly from his diary notes but tainted nevertheless by the exaggeratedly somber mood of morbid despair which he exteriorized in his senti- mental description of his visit, is contained in the first part of *Suprêmes Visions d'Orient,* published in 1921. Despite the fact that Istanbul is changing—there are now barracks, an electrical factory, and an American school where once the tombs of Mahomet II dominated the Bosphorus, the old wooden houses of Beïcos are to be replaced by modern ones, people are beginning to wear cheaper Western clothes (even the Sultan, Mahomet V, with whom Loti has an audience), the elaborate caïques on the Bosphorus are giving way to European speedboats, and the cypress trees, cemeteries, and stray dogs are fast vanishing from the city scene—Loti seeks to surround himself with as much of the Islamic life of old Turkey as possible.

During his fortnight's stay with the Count and Countess Ostrorog[3] near Candilli on the more traditional Asiatic side of the Bosphorus, he enjoys watching the caïques decorated with gold and *verroterie* and laden with fish and melons gliding down the Bosphorus and visits the local village to sit in a café with white-bearded old men in their red and green robes smoking narghiles and watching the dervishes going to the mosque or the Anatolian peasants selling their grapes to groups of veiled women. He goes, too, to the villages of Canlidja and Anatoli-Hissar, where life has changed little and he is once again fascinated by the men in their robes and turbans, the veils of the women, the citadel walls of Mahomet, and the local saint's tomb, where he lights a candle in appreciation of the traditional Islamic existence he so admires there; and when he finally moves to Istanbul itself and is let an apartment in the Moslem sector of the city, Eskiali-Djiami, by a Turkish naval officer,[4] he immediately has it furnished in Oriental style and enjoys immensely sitting in the nearby cafés, chatting with the imams there or dreamily awaiting with them the call to prayer in the mosque opposite, where they often invite him to accompany them.

Despite his attempts to immerse himself in the traditional life of old Turkey of the past and regain his enjoyment of it, Loti's stay in Istanbul is depicted as essentially lonely and melancholy: When he visits Beïcos and is recognized by the café owner there, he is reminded of when he once came there with his ship's crew; and when he sees the valley nearby and, later, the Eaux Douces, he recalls his meetings with the three *désenchantées*, whom he tries to rediscover, but in vain. Above all, it is his visits to the tomb of Aziyadé, now so weathered in the decaying cemetery that his key no longer opens it and still containing the thistles he left there the last time, which impress him with a sense of time passing and imminent mortality; this is emphasized even more when he takes his son at great risk into the sacrosanct mosque at Eyub, where he once lived, to see the gilded tombs of Mahomet II's court, and to Aziyadé's tomb, and when he soon afterward falls ill.[5] When his condition allows him to leave the French hospital at Pera after three weeks, he cannot return to his apartment in the Moslem sector of the city and is offered accommodation in the country home of the French consul Alphonse Cillière at Ortakeni on the Bosphorus. Muffled up against the chill of autumn and left alone watching the last dahlias and asters of the season dying and the last caïques gliding over the water, Loti feels, as he listens to the muezzin's call to prayer evoking memories of his past, that his end is near: "I watch the decline of the summer, of the Orient, and of my own life; it is the end of everything."

Such is Loti's self-pitying portrait of himself and his surroundings painted in the colors of his own despair. His son's departure to France to do his military service and the difficulties involved in his walking further than the nearest café, the coming of winter and closing of the shops and cafés on the coast, and his symbolic melancholy at the thought that his memories of Istanbul as well as the Islamic heritage of old Turkey are receding farther into the past eventually encourage him to return to France in late October, 1910.

III   Turquie Agonisante

This stay in Turkey was not, however, Loti's last, as he himself had imagined during his illness, when he so passionately embraced Aziyadé's tomb and made out his will in the hospital. Indeed, it was but the beginning of a new aspect of his association with that country. As the European powers and the Balkan states intrigued to despoil the moribund Ottoman empire, already internally ravaged by the clashes of the Sultanate and the Young Turks and the uprisings of the rebel bands of *comitadjis,* of its power and influence, so Loti became more and more adamant in his defense of this ally of France; and the more anti-Turk Europe became, the more polemical and propagandist did Loti become in his appeals and protests on behalf of the land of Aziyadé and the *désenchantées;* for an attack on Turkey was one on the poetic vision of that country reflecting his own mood and outlook which Loti had cherished ever since his first visit, partly as a fetish for his own security,[6] in his exotic cult of himself. He would defend it to the last with all the vehemence of his despair, even if it meant distorting the truth to vindicate his symbolic image of it. On 3 January 1912 he protested in *Le Figaro* at the Italian taking of Tripoli in September, 1911, comparing the suddenness of the attack, the inequality in arms of the parties involved, and the heroic and desperate fight of the Arabs, particularly the fishermen on the Red Sea, against Italian brutality, to a panther's attack on a buffalo he once witnessed, and asserting that Italy should give up her prey and not disembowel it with the other Great Powers. On his return from the cascades of lights, skyscrapers, and crowds of reporters of New York, where he had stayed briefly in September, 1912, to see the rehearsals and opening of George Tyler's production of his play about the Empress of China, *La Fille du Ciel,* at the Century Theater,[7] Loti was to take up Turkey's cause again in the First Balkan War, which broke out in October. His views on the war, first published in the current press, appeared in the volume *Turquie Agonisante* of 1913.

As the front cover, showing a horribly mutilated Turkish soldier, implies and the preface clearly states, Loti aims to correct the reputation of the Turks as the sole barbarians and inform the French public of their true nature. In "Les Turcs Massacrent," Loti explains that the Turks are a quiet, religious, family- and animal-loving people and that if they have reacted against aggression with the same brutality as the European powers have displayed in Africa and Asia it is because they have been provoked like Spanish bulls in a bull-ring; they have been brought to taking desperate measures because of their abandonment by their allies, including France, and because Turkish power has been undermined by modern innovations and Armenian-Christian infiltration into the Moslem army's ranks. Instead of trying to preserve Turkey as the last refuge of the Islamic heritage of simplicity, peace, sobriety, and prayer in the modern world of factories, alcoholism, railways and warfare, just as parks are preserved in industrial cities, the innocent, virtually unarmed, and much maligned Turks are being mowed down by the sophisticated weapons of the Bulgars and Greeks, and the European powers just greedily await the spoils of this political staghunt. France and her allies have been misled by Bulgar propaganda into thinking of the Turks as guilty of vast massacres and convinced by their King, Ferdinand of Coburg, that Balkan aggression on Turkey is part of a Christian crusade there.

Loti points out, however, in "Lettres sur la Guerre des Balkans," that a Bulgar-Greek victory will also be one for the Orthodox Church and this in turn will by its fanaticism prevent the work of Catholic Frenchmen in Turkey, where France has already invested some $2\frac{1}{2}$ million francs in social welfare and commerce. Furthermore, the conduct of Turkey's attackers has been far from Christian. Quoting the letters and accounts of people living in or knowing Turkey well, Loti tries to prove that it is not the Turks, as the French press gives out, who are massacring whole villages and committing atrocities, but the Bulgars, Serbs and Greeks; he claims the Bulgars have massacred forty thousand Turks and been guilty of rape and mutilation; and in "Massacres de Macédonie et Massacres d'Arménie," he asserts that Turkish reprisals in 1896 during the Armenian revolts were not as terrible as the recent massacres of Turks, reports of which are just reaching France. According to Loti, Europe has willingly accepted the wicked, cowardly Ferdinand of Coburg's idea of a crusade and allegations of Turkish atrocities as part of the political conspiracy to bring about the downfall of Turkey's Islamic culture and power.

IV   Suprêmes Visions d'Orient, 1913

In August, 1913, Loti returned to Turkey for five weeks and was accorded a royal welcome by the people he had so passionately supported almost alone in France. At Istanbul a large crowd greets him on his arrival; at Candilli, where he stays again, he is taken on board an exquisite caïque furnished with cushions and carpets and entertained by the villagers with music and fireworks; the Sultan gives him his jeweled watch and chain as a token of friendship and provides him with precious antique utensils and bibelots from the Old Seraglio as well as a table of Sultan Abdul Aziz for the apartment he rents for three weeks in the old sector of the city; the Sultan also holds a banquet in the grand, old-style manner within the bastions of the Old Seraglio in honor of his guest and a special theater performance is arranged, at which Loti is given a standing ovation by the audience; and at Adrianople the whole city turns out to greet him, he is driven in procession through the streets to the sound of the *Marseillaise,* and is accommodated under close guard in the former headquarters of the Bulgarian general who had taken the city in March that year.

As well as finding to his delight that life in Turkey has barely

changed and the mosques he visits have not lost their charm—he
virtually panics at one point when he goes to the wrong cemetery
and cannot discover Aziyadé's tomb, which he fears has been removed
by progressive political elements in the country—Loti, above all,
hears on this visit the full horror of what he had suspected in *Turquie
Agonisante:* the massacre of Turks by Bulgars. He learns from
survivors and eyewitnesses how the Bulgars destroyed mosques,
soiled their minarets, slew whole villages in Thrace, raped women,
disposed of the bodies of their victims in rivers and wells, and mutilated others by cutting off their ears, hands or breasts, and gouging
out their eyes. From a Greek, Pandelli, who escaped being drowned
in the river with dozens of other bound prisoners, Loti learns how
homes were pillaged and burnt, women and girls raped, and their
menfolk starved and bayoneted; and he expresses his horror at the
atrocities committed by the Greeks, too, at Yalova and protests at
the murder of sixty French sailors at Athens by the wicked scheming
of the Greek King and Queen. These revelations not only confirm
Loti's earlier suspicions, but also make him cling all the more to the
old, Islamic Ottoman Turkey he loves. He knows, as news of the
Great Powers' division of Turkey at the peace conference after the
second Balkan War reaches him, that, with Balkan ambitions and
the progressive Young Turks' demands, the country could no longer
exist as it was; but he enjoys for the last time living as an Oriental in
the old quarter of Istanbul opposite the house at Eski where he first
lived as a midshipman, having Aziyadé's tomb redecorated as if to
renew his contact with the past, seeing his old friends such as the Os-
trorogs and the Sultan's sons, and witnessing the magnificent luxury
of the moribund Ottoman Empire before it too, like Loti and his
past, is overtaken by the modern world.

V *The First World War*

While the traditional life and glorious past of the Ottoman
empire were being eroded from within and from outside in the cause
of "progress," a relative of Ferdinand of Coburg, the German
Kaiser, was preparing his own military type of modern crusade to
enlighten the rest of Europe on such matters. If Turkey's fate
represented for Loti that of his own outlook and exotic cult in the
modern world, the sophisticated warfare of Germany and cata-

clysmic turmoil of the First World War were condemned by him as the result of Europe's overdevelopment and departure from her simple traditional way of life—a process similar to that in his own career, as he explained in "Vertige" (in *Quelques Aspects du Vertige Mondial*). Loti was in the seclusion of his family house at Rochefort when news of the German invasion of Luxemburg first disturbed the drowsy peace of the summer in early August, 1914; he could hardly believe, when all around him was so quiet and normal, that anyone could be embarking on such a dangerous course of action or indeed dare to make such a move in the present situation of vast military buildups. But when his son joins the 44th Battery of the 3rd Artillery soon after war is declared, Loti too desires to serve his country and even die for it; he puts on his tropical uniform from Saigon and signs on at the Prefecture in Rochefort on 3 August just as he so often did in his youth before embarking on a voyage; it was as if the war was offering him fresh hope of adventure in the declining years of his retirement.

Because of his age (64 years), and his poor health, he was given a temporary job at the arsenal in Rochefort. This clearly did not satisfy his desire for action and he protested to the authorities on 18 August, asking for a post where he could be of greater service to his country. On 1 September he was sent home, but on 1 February the following year he was offered the post of aide to the military governor of Paris, General Galliéni, after serving there already in the intervening months as a liaison officer; and in October, 1915, he undertook certain missions for the War Ministry while being attached for a year to the headquarters of the Groupe d'Armées du Centre of Generals Pétain, Castelnau, and Langle de Cary. In June, 1916, Loti asked his friend Louis Barthou to find out through an acquaintance in the War Ministry if he could join General Franchet d'Esperey's headquarters in Alsace so that he could write on the War at first hand. This he was allowed to do and he spent the next year—apart from an unsuccessful trip to Madrid in the summer of 1916 to seek Spanish support for the war—doing reconnaissance work on the use of artillery, bridge construction, explosives, and weather conditions for air warfare, and writing propagandist articles on his experiences in *L'Illustration*.

From now on the venom of Loti's polemic was turned from the despoilers of Turkey to the enemies of France;[8] from Ferdinand

of Coburg to his relation, the Kaiser; from Bulgars and Greeks
to the Germans. And instead of painting the exotic, Loti used his
talents to describe and appeal for the men and women fighting for
his homeland against its invaders.

VI   La Hyène Enragée

Loti's early impressions of the War—his hatred of the Germans
and admiration for the courage of the French—are found in
La Hyène Enragée, published after censorship in 1916. Quoting
Vellius Paterculus, Maria Theresa, Goethe, and Schopenhauer on
the hypocrisy, ferocity, and stupidity of the Germans, which he sees
epitomized in the Hohenzollerns and their latest progeny, the
Kaiser, with his viperine eyes and treacherous, grotesque smile,
Loti stresses the barbarism of this "cretinous creature with neither
brain nor soul" by describing the scenes he witnesses at the Front
and in Belgium in 1914–15. It is the savage Germans who have
carved the countryside of Northern France into miles of trench
corridors and forced young Frenchmen to lead a cold, wet,
troglodyte existence in them in the middle of a misty, empty
landscape and under constant bombardment; it is the invaders
who have turned peaceful villages like Soissons into silent
ruins and their leader, "he whose blood-sucking tentacles one
is sure to find drawing their fill in the wounds of whatever country
on the face of the earth, the great organizer of worldwide massacres, the king of swindlers, and overlord of the abattoir and
charnelhouse," who has sanctioned the pillaging and ransacking
of homes just as he did in Peking; it is the enemy who has transformed the spring landscape of gentle sunlight and melting
snow into a scene of horror with men standing knee-deep in
mud in their trenches listening to a distant cannonade and
waiting, others searching the skies for a new species of bird of
prey whose potential is much more fatal to humankind than any
creature of Nature, and yet others whose blood spatters the
snow or whose remains are heaped beneath it; and it is the Germans
who have converted war from being an honorable combat into a pre-
historic-like struggle without pity or chivalry using the most
inhuman weapons and tactics.

Loti's indignation reaches its peak both when he shows the

results of the shelling of the medieval basilica and Flemish Drapers Hall of Ypres and the delicate masonry of the historic Cathedral of Rheims and when he describes the inferno-like scene in a dark, improvised hospital still under enemy fire where men are being treated after a poison-gas attack. By depicting such atrocities— the smashing of the stained-glass windows at Rheims, the shattered paintings and carvings of Ypres, the swollen bodies of the gassed men—Loti hopes to convince anyone or any country with a pro-German or neutral view to realize the barbarism of the enemy in destroying irreplaceable works of art which neither Time nor Man has so far done, and using such horrible weapons against their fellowmen, as well as their futile cruelty in shelling cathedrals and hospitals.

If the Germans are wicked and treacherous, then those who are fighting them are all the more to be admired for their courage and endurance. Loti's mission from the French President to King Albert of Belgium in March, 1915, and his meeting with the young Queen reveal to him the determined resistance that country is putting up against its invaders in the worst of circumstances; his visits to the surprisingly cheerful men at the Front to whom he distributes cigarettes and newspapers, his meetings with those manning the antiaircraft installations he inspects, and his acquaintance with medical and charitable helpers inspire him with the greatest admiration of their unity and determination despite their differences of social class and often nationality. He urges, for example, that the six thousand sailors who held the Germans at Dixmunde for three weeks without proper supplies and gear should receive the *croix de guerre;* he is grateful for American participation in the war; and he appeals on behalf of various organizations to provide ambulances in the field, money for survivors, and help to the blinded. His appeal for the latter, entitled *Georges Lormont,* and appearing like many others in *Quelques Aspects du Vertige Mondial,* tells the tragic tale of a young man injured in the war who recovers only to discover that he will be blind for life, and is one of Loti's most moving pieces of writing. These sufferings and the death of innocent young Frenchmen such as the son of his friend Louis Barthou, to whom the volume is dedicated, and the three men whose graves Loti and his sailor valet Osman seek out on a misty, cold day near the German lines, only

1 138   PIERRE LOTI

make Loti all the more determined that the Gorgon-like Kaiser who so desires to bring "progress" to his neighbors should get his desserts together with his countrymen who blindly follow him.

VII   L'Horreur Allemande

Further examples of Loti's condemnation and mockery of the Kaiser's ambitious crusade and of German stupidity and barbarism are found in *L'Horreur Allemande* published in 1918. His descriptions of French villages in ruins, their houses and churches gaping and ransacked, their belongings scattered, the fields nearby full of craters and barbed-wire coils, trees cut down, and bridges and factories destroyed are filled with his indignation and desire that such savagery should not be forgotten, and also with a tender pity instilled through his personification of the ruined homes:

I should think that this evening my eyes are gazing upon a scene never witnessed before, a scene at which one cannot bear to look; a wave of indignation and hate rises in me. . . . Farms, orchards, hamlets, villages or smallish towns, everything from top to bottom has been laid waste in such a way that nothing is any more of use and repairs are no longer possible, for all the walls have been razed right to the ground and not a brick remains in place; what determination and devilish patience they must have had! All along what were once streets, the few remains of the fronts of houses stare at one through the great gaps that were their windows but are now without frames or shutters and look like eyeless skulls. Occasionally roofs or ceilings that have been ripped out come crashing down and their beams are left sticking up in the air like the long arms of some prisoner begging for mercy and raised toward the sky as if asking the heavens to be his witness. Here and there, Kaiser Wilhelm's band of gorillas have scrawled before they left some curse which makes one shrug one's shoulders as one passes by its utter senselessness.

The volume also records Loti's second meeting with the King of Belgium, to whom he delivers a message from his commanding officer, General Franchet d'Esperey, and with the Queen, whom he finds playing with some war orphans and accompanies on a pleasant walk through some woods nearby. *L'Horreur Allemande* describes, too, Loti's further visit to an even more dilapidated Rheims and his stay in Italy from 24 July to late August, 1917. Here, he admires the gallant efforts made by the Italians against the Austrians in the Dolomites and is fascinated by the Jules Verne type of battle being fought high up on the snow-covered slopes and crags under heavy camouflage with cannons and shells stored in the mountain caverns; he is amazed how the Italians have been able to construct roads round the mountains and capture Austrian positions on them under enemy fire. After a stop at the ancient basilica at Aquila, a meeting with the King of Italy in his villa, and a visit to the actress Eleonora Duse entertaining the troops there, Loti stays at the Hotel Danieli in Venice, where he is given the suite George Sand and Alfred de Musset once shared and recalls his own acquaintance there with the Queen of Rumania. His description of wartime Venice—the Doges Palace and St. Marks muffled up in protective material and scaffolding against incendiary bomb attacks, their paintings and other precious furnishings hidden away, many other churches and palaces of artistic value being used as hospitals lying in ruins after air attack, and the streets and canals deserted despite the summer heat—reveal once more his condemnation of the senselessness of modern warfare and the horror of its sophisticated weapons. The German invaders are, however, being gradually put to flight in France and there is thus an opportunity at last for Europe to rid itself of the treacherous scheming and inhuman barbarism of the Kaiser:

Oh no! now that the German beast is at last gasping for breath and lies bleeding from its wounds, do not, for God's sake, give it the respite it is hoping for. The German beast is doomed if we continue our efforts and so is the Kaiser who excites and spurs it on like the picadors with their horses charging at the bull! Let us sacrifice our belongings, our well-being, our lives and those of our dearest ones right to the end, let us make the supreme effort, so that we may pass on to our children a Europe, covered in ruins and cemeteries, horribly ravaged and denuded of the artistic treasures of its past, maybe, but at least a Europe where there will be no murderous Kaiser!

Soon after Loti returned from his mission to Italy to the headquarters at Vic-sur-Aisne near Soissons, where he had lived since being transferred to the Groupe d'Armées de l'Est, he fell ill and was sent home by the headquarters' physician Dr. Bué. His rather lonely life among military personnel in miserable and often unhealthy living conditions, as well as the fatigue of his missions and his writing, had undermined his frail constitution and rendered his small frame more haggard than ever.[9] On 15 March 1918, he was demobilized, but he struggled against such a surrender to his age and health and as soon as he had recovered a little in late April, 1918, he was back voluntarily at General Franchet d'Esperey's headquarters near the Front at Epernay. Unfortunately, despite his will to carry on the fight, his nerves and constitution could not endure the tension of the fighting and the dampness, and he was again sent home on 27 May 1918. By 11 November 1919 his name was definitively removed from the reserve list. The moment he had feared most had come—he had not been granted an honorable death at the Front and was now left, alone and ailing, without any mission to fulfill or role to play, to languish and await death in the silence of the old house at Rochefort among the relics of his past.[10] The fate of another country continued, however, to concern Loti in these post war years—that of Turkey.

VIII   La Mort de notre chère France en Orient

When the new Sultan of Turkey, Mahomet VI, signed an armistice with the Allies in late October, 1918, just before Germany capitulated in Western Europe, his country was exhausted and his empire virtually lost. Such a condition encouraged Turkey's despoilers to try and gain now by treaty what they had attempted to claim before the war by diplomatic intrigue; the "sick man of Europe" was to be killed by his doctors. The terms imposed on Turkey by the armistice, the occupation of the Straits, Istanbul, and some other areas, and the proposals for the Treaty of Sèvres of 1920—Turkey's empire was to be divided into largely British protectorates, Greece was to acquire Izmir and Eastern Thrace, and the Sultan was to become a mere puppet under the power of the Allies—were obviously distasteful to Loti; his sense of shame at Clemenceau's abandonment of France's old ally and resignation to the terms being imposed on the Turks by the British under Lloyd George is expressed in the volume of newspaper articles and letters entitled *La Mort de notre chère France en Orient* published in 1920.

As elsewhere, Loti maintains that the Turks are a kind, family-loving people, whose country is a last haven of peace and prayer in the modern world, and he quotes dozens of letters from people who have come into contact with them to support his point. In "Les Massacres d'Arménie," he adds that if they did massacre Armenians it was because they had been provoked by internal revolts incited by foreign agents and alarmed by the ferocity of the Armenians' attack on Istanbul; the Turks are, in any case, not the only country to have massacred people in history and the Armenians are not themselves guiltless in this respect despite all their hypocritical propaganda to the contrary. France should help her old ally and regain her prestige in the Arab world; she should resist British expansion in the Middle East and championing of Greece; she should protest at the British occupation of Istanbul and the Greek seizure of Izmir and claims on Thrace; she should ensure that President Wilson's twelfth principle on the sovereignty of nations according to nationality is applied to Turkey—Izmir is Turkish despite the nucleus of Greeks around the port and the people of Thrace lead a traditional Turkish life—and ask him to condemn also the Greeks burning Turkish houses in Istanbul, when he warns the Turks to stop massacring Armenians in Anatolia. But France has taken none of these steps; British force has ousted French prestige; they have occupied Istanbul, arrested many of Loti's supporters, rendered the Sultan powerless, condemned the nationalist forces of Mustapha Kemel, allowed Greece to take Izmir, and—it is rumored—signed a secret treaty with Turkey upholding the Sultan in return for rights in his empire.

France should go into mourning, as the Turks have done, for allowing such a tragedy. Unfortunately, not everyone shared Loti's idealistic views, which were seen as an old man's sentimental hysteria, and many pamphlets against him were published by Armenians and others involved in their cause. The Allies' dismemberment of Turkey thus continued.

IX Prime Jeunesse

The agony of the land of Aziyadé virtually coincided with that of Loti himself; its insecurity both caused and reflected Loti's own. His last two years or more are spent quietly by his fireside or more often in his bedroom on the second floor of the old house at Rochefort; as well as his secretary Gaston Mauberger, his majordomo Pierre, his valet Lucien Labéguerie, and his sailor friends Osman Daney, Edmond Gueffier and Simon Saucès, he often has his son with him and together they compose two biographical works on his early life,

Prime Jeunesse, published in 1919, and *Un Jeune Officier Pauvre*
completed by Samuel Loti-Viaud after his father's death in 1923. Both
works continue the story of Loti's youth: The first follows on from
Le Roman d'un Enfant and deals with the years 1863–1867; the
second, based on the period 1868–1878, uses Loti's diary to record
his early years in the navy from the "Jean Bart" to the "Tonnerre"
and his romances in Senegal and Turkey.

Prime Jeunesse, dedicated to Loti's sister Marie who had died in
September, 1908, and described by him at one point as "a long epitaph
on some deeply revered gravestones," is not only a sentimental account
of his life at home, his visit to Oleron, the engagement and marriage
of his sister, the deaths of Lucie and Gustave, the family's financial
straits, and his experiences in Paris and on the *"Borda",* but also
Loti's last attempt to cling to the relics of his past. The old house at
Rochefort, the pond Gustave built for his small brother, the fountain
where Marie and her future husband decided to marry, the flowers
planted by Tante Claire, the woods of Limoise, and the dragonflies
in the clearing where Loti met a gypsy girl still exist, but the people
associated with them are all gone or dead now. Only Nature continues its eternal process of destruction—here, of the bodies of those
who have died—and of re-creation—in this case, the flowers
and insects of the past. *Prime Jeunesse* is then not merely a nostalgic, retrospective evocation of the simple innocence of Loti's
vanished childhood, as was *Le Roman d'un Enfant,* but a melancholy,
even morbid account of the later, year-by-year dissolution of the
world of his early childhood with the knowledge that it is now,
with the imminence of his own death, about to pass away forever;
hence his desire to evoke the further memories of these years, to
describe and name his childhood aunts and girlfriend in Paris,
and publish the text of Gustave's last letters to the family and
his description in his diary from that time of his days with Lucie
at Limoise.

X   *Loti's Death*

Although extremely weak and haggard in his last years, Loti was
able to witness his son's marriage to the daughter of Vice-Admiral
Charlier on 12 May 1920 and receive the Grand Croix of the Légion
d'Honneur in December, 1921, as a result of a petition to the government signed by Pierre Louÿs, Victor Margueritte, Rosny *aîné,* Pierre

Mille, Pierre Benoît, Cassagnac, Courteline, Bourget, and Louis Barthou. When his friend Farrère visits him at Rochefort in late December, 1921, in order to entertain on his behalf some Turkish guests who have come to present him with a carpet made by war orphans, Loti is so frail as to inspire pity and has to be carried down the stairs to take leave of his visitors; he had not lost any of his intelligence, however, and enjoys hearing his guests speaking Turkish and trying to converse with them in the language of Aziyadé.[11] Loti's condition continues to deteriorate during 1922, as news of the Sultan's exile to Malta and the rise of Mustapha Kemal arrives, and on 23 June he suffers a severe stroke that for a while deprives him of virtually all movement and speech. Later that year he writes to Mme Adam, now eighty-seven years old, telling her how his indignation over Turkey's fate has exhausted him and urgently requesting her to visit him before it is too late; this she does on 28 April 1923.[12]

On 5 June that year, Loti and his doctors decide that a change of air might be beneficial and he makes the tiring journey down to his House of the Solitary at Hendaye; the weather is fine and Loti enjoys pottering in his garden there. On 8 June, however, he falls ill and the next day his three doctors from Hendaye, Rochefort, and Paris are summoned to his bedside; they bleed him but he loses consciousness soon after midday. The following day, at about four o'clock in the afternoon, Loti passes away, surrounded by his family including the small grandson named after him.[13]

As death had been in Loti's thoughts for so long, it is not surprising that he had made provision for his funeral and burial long before the event. As early as the summer of 1919[14] he had visited the mayor on Oleron and written to the pastor of Rochefort to ask that he be buried in the garden of his ancestors' home on the Isle of Oleron, which he had acquired and inspected with his son in April, 1899, his gravestone be a simple one with just his name on it, and the service be a private one. He had even requested that his coffin should be as thin as possible and a hole be made in his coffin before burial so that the earth might penetrate fully into it; his *pelota* glove, an embroidered Turkish scarf of Aziyadé, and a small shovel given him by his Tante Claire were to be buried with him; and his grave was to be closed to the public and looked after by ten people he appointed.[15] Apart from family heirlooms, nearly all his belongings were to be burnt to avoid their profanation after his death.[16]

CHAPTER 9

Conclusion

I Loti and his Age

THE impact of Loti's novels and the receptivity of the public to his exoticism can be estimated by the hundreds of editions that many of his works went into and the number of translations, dramatizations, and even operas that were made of them.[1] If the author of *Aziyadé* and *Madame Chrysanthème* was so popular, it was because, like Kipling, he was so representative of his age. As a naval officer, he stood for the expansion of French power overseas, and by his writing exploited the patriotic fervor that this aroused under Jules Ferry and that found expression in a series of World Exhibitions. As a world traveler he appealed to the desire of people to see new places and find new inspiration that earlier took Goethe and Byron abroad and later seized a host of writers and painters, as well as an increasingly large number of Cooks tourists, who wanted to follow in their own small way in the steps of the great explorers or, like Henry James's American expatriates, sought contact with Culture away from home. As a collector of exotic bric-à-brac, the owner of a house with Chinese and Arab rooms, an enthusiast of foreign fauna, an artist of faraway people and places and an observer of their customs and dress, Loti was typical of his time: an age that, following the rococo and neo-classical exoticism of the eighteenth century and the archeological finds of the Napoleonic campaigns, was increasingly fascinated by the new, strange world of overseas; a public who wanted to grasp it for themselves by stocking their museums, zoos, botanic gardens and bookcases at home, by purchasing Islamic and Oriental bibelots by the dozen, prizing pictures and books of the exotically colorful, and trying to imitate foreign habits and styles in items of dress and furnishing. These were the years of Livingstone, Rhodes, Marchand, Galliéni, Gordon, and young Churchill, when vogues and taste for the exotic passed from one strange, exciting land to another as, thanks to faster communications, each was revealed by colonialists, explorers, or travelers and made known to the public at home as it was opened up;

145

and this change in taste was reflected in the arts and literature.[2] Such then was the evolution of taste of the period that witnessed Lord Leighton's Arabian Hall, Alma-Tadema's art, Leconte de Lisle's poetry, Goncourt's essays on Japanese painting, Debussy's music, Gilbert and Sullivan's *Mikado* and Puccini's *Madame Butterfly.*

Exoticism in literature is an attempt to transform reality by having recourse to the sensations of strangeness produced by the exotic; but at the same time as seeking to transform reality and even stressing this transformation by the extreme nature of the sensations of strangeness evoked, the writer can stand back from his exoticism and even be unmoved by its transforming influence on his imagination. The exotic is therefore the means of escape of the rebel and the refuge of the voyeur.

The exoticists of the nineteenth century preferred the exciting variety and color of life overseas to the monotonous social uniformity and increasing industrial mechanization of bourgeois life in France; they preferred the epic richness of history to the banal dullness of the present, as did Hugo and Mérimée; they longed in their eclectic skepticism for other spiritual and moral ideals to replace the iconoclastic values of commerce and science of the world around them; they sought in their social isolation the transcendental supremacy of the mystic, as did Nerval and Baudelaire, and dreamed of the pleasures of kings and queens; and socially inactive and morally impotent, they evoked, as did Gautier and Flaubert, masochistic visions of the Fatal Woman and indulged in every type of perverse eroticism.[3] In short, they desired a new set of spiritual and moral values, a new idealism, to replace those values undermined by social change and scientific innovation. The means of expressing the exotic thus became more and more refined and varied after 1870 as the rift between writer and society became wider, culminating in the nervous impressionism of the Goncourts, the decadent dandyism of Huysmans' *A Rebours,* and the hermeticism of the Symbolists.[4] Pierre Loti's use of the exotic reflects a similar aesthetic reaction to his immediate reality and the spiritual and moral climate of his age.

II *Loti's Exoticism*

Loti's disillusionment with the world after a childhood filled with the tenderness of his mother and family, the stability of their

Protestant heritage, and the innocent simplicity of his early friendships and love of Nature, his intellectual sophistication and loss of faith, his shyness outside his family and small stature—all made him long to escape his present situation and regain the security, naturalness, and innocence of his past. His personal sense of inadequacy and desire to find an idealism and image of himself he could accept were, with the disillusioned skepticism he shared with his generation, the conditions that nurtured the escapist exoticism of the Romantic social rebel and aesthetic voyeur.

But, unlike many of the Romantics, Loti actually travelled overseas; his exoticism was thus a realistic but nonetheless detachedly aesthetic attempt at spiritual and emotional self-completion through a retrospective cult of his romanticized experiences of the simplicity, ideals, faith, and customs of other people in other lands where the skepticism and sophistication of Europe had not yet penetrated. The countries he described, the tales of the lovers and sailors or soldiers he told, are then merely functional in his evocation of the feelings and values associated with his emotional cult and spiritual quest just as a love poet may use his relations with a mistress as an exteriorization of his personality and view of life; hence Loti's disregard in his works for motive, plot, and characters' psychology and his reliance on impressionistic tableaux, sentimental situations, and actual experiences all related to himself.[5] He was seeking to turn back the clock of his civilized existence and return to that antediluvian state of evolution in his childhood, which he admired in Nature; his impressionism and fetishism,[6] his makeup and stress on physical fitness, his love of costumes and disguises, and his masochistic, neo-homosexual relationships with men and neo-filial or fraternal attitude to women were all part of the cult of himself he practiced with a neo-religious fervor in order to escape his present self and reflect his desire to stop time and retreat into his childhood situation of simplicity, stability, and vitality founded on family security, faith, and proximity to Nature. The failure of these attempts to provide permanent escapist relief and the increasing sophistication of Europe together with its Westernization of its colonies overseas prevented Loti from attaining what was an impossible goal.

The aesthetic escapism of Loti's exoticism did not then solve the personal problem and spiritual quest underlying it any more than other escapist eccentricities of his contemporaries in dandyism,

148 PIERRE LOTI

perversion, or mysticism. His works, with their mixture of exoticism and traditionalism, of skepticism and a desire for faith, and of impressionistic realism and poetic imagination, are typical of the moral conflict of the period that witnessed the spiritual reaction against the stress on the physical aspects of life of Zola's Naturalism, the formulation of Symbolism with its emphasis on the inner man, and the concomitant religious revival of the turn of the century.[7]

For, although Loti wanted to appear as simple and unsophisticated a writer as possible as part of his spiritual quest and claimed therefore that he had read little[8] and disliked the intellectual climate of Parisian society, his works show that same moral development in thought and approach as those of his contemporaries. The exoticism of his early novels is every bit as skeptical in its idealistic mood and sophisticated artistically in its documented realism and impressionism as the works of Flaubert or the Goncourts; the implied eroticism of his early works is reminiscent of Zola; the "sentimental egoism"[9] of his personal impressions and moods can be compared to the dilettantist egocentricity of the early Bourget and Barrès; his pessimism in *Fleurs d'Ennui* is very much like the Baudelairean idealism current in the early 1880's on account of the influence of Schopenhauer and Wagner; the praise of the primitive lives and faith of simple people, such as *Pasquala Ivanovitch, Mon Frère Yves* and *Pêcheur d'Islande* conveyed, the emphasis on compassion in *Le Livre de la Pitié et de la Mort* and *Matelot* and on the values of childhood, and the portrait of *L'Exilée* are highly reminiscent of similar novels inspired at this time by the work of the Russian writers, whose Christian altruistic example E. M. de Vogüe had recommended in opposition to current pessimistic and dilettantist trends in his *Du Roman Russe* (1886); Loti's speech to the Académie[10] echoes exactly the reaction against Naturalism and vague idealism of the late 1880's and early 1890's, while his *fin de siècle* depiction of Carmen Silva and Venice with its sense of Occidental decay mirrored the spiritual agony of European sophistication also described by Barrès and Mann; his religious quest overseas of the last decade of the century parallels that of his contemporaries such as Zola, Bourget, Brunetière, Huysmans, and Rod in their attraction to Rome; his studies of his Huguenot ancestors in *Judith Renaudin* and of the traditional life of the Basques and the issues of social *déracinement* in *Ramuntcho* reflect the same search for faith and stable social values in so far unsophisticated communities and the historic heritages they upheld as can be found in Bazin, Bourget, Barrès, and Rod; his sense of the decline of the old world of the past with the rise of modern civilization was common to most pre-1914 writers; his *Désenchantées,* based on the issues of women's education and marriage in Turkey, has affinities with the current *roman social* being produced on such issues in France in the first decade of the new century when interest in traditionalism was turned by political events into questioning of social institutions; and the political bias of Loti's last works can be found in the dominating polemic of other writers just before and during the war.

It is because his works, as idiosyncratic as they may appear, were closely linked nevertheless to the fundamental evolution of the moral thought of the period that they appealed to the contemporary literary world just as they did to the general public who could indulge particularly in the tear-jerking, Puccinian sentimentality as well as in the colorful evocativeness of the escapist exoticism he offered them.

For over thirty years Loti remained the camera lens through which Frenchmen viewed the world overseas and watched the growth of their empire; he showed them what life was like in the French navy, colonies, and spheres of interest in the world; he exploited their taste for the exotic in an age of exploration and commercial and colonial expansion and in a society of increasingly industrial complexity and through the apparent simplicity and personal authenticity of his indulgent sophistication. He also appealed to them by stimulating impressions of the exotic latent feelings they also experienced: the sentimental melancholy and despair of his anguish at the passing of his world of the past and the hopes he cherished that some of its naturalness, simplicity, and faith would still survive the advent of modern civilization. Long before the creations of Hollywood and the present-day treks of young people away from civilization,[11] Loti allowed his readers to go off with him to distant lands, which at first evoked the emotions and ideals of a past he sought to regain and later reflected its decline and agony in a present age he could no longer escape.

Notes and References

Chapter One

1. See the genealogical tables and other details of Loti's ancestors in Odette Valence & Samuel Viaud, *La Famille de Pierre Loti* (Paris: C. Lévy, 1940), pp. 8–9 *et seq*. Portraits of Loti's immediate family were painted by his sister Marie and are reproduced in N. Serban, *Pierre Loti, sa vie—son oeuvre* (Paris: Presses Françaises, 1924), pp. 16–17.

2. For pictures of and details on Loti's association with Oleron, see Yvan Delteil, *L'Ile d'Oleron* (La Rochelle: Rose des Vents, 1935) 101 pp.; and for the history of the Renaudins on Oleron, see F. de Vaux de Foletier, "Les Ancêtres de Pierre Loti," *Revue Hebdomadaire*, 29 January 1927, pp. 597–608.

3. O. Valence & S. Viaud, *op. cit.*, p. 12.

4. Edmund d'Auvergne, *Pierre Loti, The Romance of a Great Writer* (London: Werner Laurie, 1926), p. 7.

5. The photographs Gustave sent home including one of his house in Papeete and details of his stay in Tahiti can be seen in *Gustave Viaud premier photographe de Tahiti*, ed. P. O'Reilly & A. Jammes (Paris: Société des Océanistes, 1964), 32 pp.

6. O. Valence & S. Viaud, *op. cit.*, p. 84.

7. L. Daudet, *Fantômes et Vivants* (Paris: Nouvelle Librairie Nationale, 1914), p. 199.

8. O. Valence & S. Viaud, *op.cit.*, p. 131.

9. P. Loti, *Correspondance Inédite, 1865–1904*, ed. N. Duvignau & N. Serban (Paris: C. Lévy, 1929), p. 86.

10. *Ibid.*, p. 107.

11. *Ibid.*, p. 19.

12. N. Serban, *op. cit.*, p. 33.

13. See M. Salomon, "Les Premières Pages de Pierre Loti," *Revue de Paris*, 15 January 1899, pp. 443–52. Loti's description of porpoises and the detail of his accounts of his visits to Paimpol and Port-Louis already indicate his later literary talent, even if he does commit the occasional spelling mistake.

14. *Correspondance Inédite*, p. 92.

15. The account of Easter Island published in *L'Illustration* in August, 1872, can be found with a few alterations in *Reflets sur la Sombre Route*.

The original text and sketches can be found in C. Wesley Bird, *Pierre Loti, Correspondant et Dessinateur 1872–89* (Paris: P. André, 1947). Only the second and third articles were actually signed; the first appeared anonymously.

Chapter Two

1. F. Brunetière, *Histoire et Littérature* (Paris: C. Lévy, 1891), II, 299–300.

2. See Mme Adam's letter to Henri d'Alméras in N. Serban, *op. cit.,* p. 246, n. 2.

3. *Lettres à Mme Juliette Adam (1880–1922)* (Paris: Plon, 1924), pp. i, iv. See also K. Millward, "Mme Adam et les Débuts de Pierre Loti," *Cahiers Pierre Loti,* September, 1960, pp. 10–15.

4. Pierre Flottes, *Le Drame Intérieur de Pierre Loti* (Paris: Courrier Littéraire, 1937), p. 82.

5. See *Journal Intime de Pierre Loti à Tahiti,* ed. E. Vedel (Tahiti, 1934), p. 289.

6. See G. Taboulet & J-Cl. Demariaux, *La Vie Dramatique de Gustave Viaud* (Paris: Scorpion, 1961), pp. 70–114. On Gustave's death, see pp. 234–50; on Julien and Marie's cult of his memory, see pp. 259–68.

7. Although Loti was to write to Marie on 19 May 1872 of his passing fancy for a Maori girl (*Correspondance Inédite,* p. 133), he later told Lucien Jousselin on 24 February 1879 on sending him the manuscript that the character of Rarahu was just a fusion of that of the Tahitian girls he had met; see Loti, *Journal Intime 1878–81* (Paris: C. Lévy, 1925), p. 62. Moreover, comparison of Loti's diary records and his novel reveals that Rarahu was often introduced into scenes where there were no girls at all present and that many of the feelings she inspires in the novel were Loti's reactions to the landscape or his relations with his friend Joseph Bernard: see R. Lefèvre, *Le Mariage de Loti* (Paris: Soc. Franç. d'Editions Littéraires et Techniques, 1935), pp. 20–67.

8. *Correspondance Inédite,* p. 120.

9. *Ibid.,* p. 136.

10. N. Serban, *op. cit.,* p. 247.

11. *Correspondance Inédite,* p. 142.

12. *Ibid.,* p. 148. A study of Loti's life in Dakar can be found in R. Mauny, "Pierre Loti au Sénégal," *Cahiers Pierre Loti,* March, 1958, pp. 12–16.

13. Loti, *Journal Intime,* pp. 33–34, 48–50. The fact that at this time Loti was still suffering from his loss of Joseph Bernard's friendship (see *Un Jeune Officier Pauvre*) might suggest that the anguish of his Dakar romance was but a disguise for his break with Bernard. Such a substitution occurred with his experiences in Tahiti: see note 7 above.

14. *Lettres à Mme Adam,* p. 10. The novel was completed in early September, 1880: see *Journal Intime,* p. 186.

15. Plumkett's annotation of the manuscript can be seen in R. Lefèvre, *En Marge de Loti* (Paris: J. Renard, 1944), pp. 61–109.

16. See Cl. Farrère, *Cent Dessins de P. Loti* (Paris: Arrault, 1948), pp. 91–120.

17. See letter to Plumkett of 4 October 1878 in *Journal Intime,* p. 32, and one to Daudet of 7 April 1880, *ibid.,* p. 127.

18. It is significant to note in this connection that in Part IV, Chapter xiii of *Aziyadé,* Loti's hero refers to Senegal as the country where he lived for a year with the brother he lost; it would seem that the Peyral-Fatou relationship was another attempt by Loti to emulate his big brother through his fiction. The fact, too, that Peyral abandons his fiancée just as Gustave had not accepted a match his mother and sister arranged for him during his absence overseas might confirm this.

19. *Correspondance Inédite,* p. 35.

20. *Lettres à Mme Adam,* p. 50.

21. Quoted in O. Valence & S. Loti-Viaud, *La Famille de P. Loti,* p. 186.

22. *Correspondance Inédite,* p. 154.

23. On Jousselin's life (1851–1932), see R. Lefèvre. *En Marge de Loti,* pp. 13–60; and Albert Jousselin, "Un Collaborateur de Pierre Loti," *Revue Maritime,* February, 1950, pp. 243–57.

24. *Journal Intime,* p. 62.

25. Cl. Farrère, *Pierre Loti quand je l'ai connu* (Paris: Amis d'Edouard, 1926), p. 20; Loti's sketches of Hakidjé, Daniel, and Eyub can be found in Farrère's *Cent Dessins de P. Loti,* pp. 129, 135, 141; photographs of Daniel and of Loti at Salonica and Istanbul are to be seen in the *Revue Maritime,* February, 1950, pp. 241, 248–49.

26. See, for example, *Cahiers Pierre Loti* (December, 1970), pp. 14–15 for his distortion of a letter to Nelly Lieutier in *Aziyadé.*

27. See O. Valence & S. Loti, *La Famille de P. Loti,* pp. 200–201. Many of Loti's early critics suggested that Aziyadé was a young man or that Loti had been the victim of a pimp but these hypotheses have since been rejected: see Pierre Briquet, *Pierre Loti et l'Orient* (Paris/Neuchâtel: Zeluck, 1945), pp. 292–349. It is probable that, as with Rarahu and Mme Chrysanthème, Aziyadé was an invented name, possibly related to the Turkish *aziz* (dear) and *yad* (memory), used to represent the romantic symbol Loti created out of his love of Turkey and his feelings for his two servant boys. The possibility of his romance, particularly in the sacred Eyub quarter, virtually banned to Europeans, is very remote: see J. Desrieux, "Loti Intime," *Le Correspondant,* 25 May 1926, pp. 529–30.

28. *Journal Intime,* p. 27.

29. The letters Loti wrote to his friend Pogarritz, Villier the Ambassador's secretary, and Hakidjé in Istanbul are found in *Un Jeune Officier Pauvre* and quoted in René Maurice, *En Marge d'Aziyadé* (Paris: Editions Universelles, 1945), pp. 49–50.

30. *Journal Intime,* p. 12.

31. See Maxime Gaucher, *Revue Politique et Littéraire,* 22 February 1879, p. 807. This was one of the first criticisms of Loti's work and earliest recognition of his talents as a writer.

32. Besides the Bible, Loti mentions in his works Homer, Virgil, Chateaubriand, Musset, Hugo, Lamartine, Feuillet, Baudelaire, and Bergson; Daudet encouraged him to read Flaubert and presumably his own work and that of Goncourt and Zola; Loti later met Renan; he also received complimentary copies of the works of contemporary writers before and after entering the Académie and visited some of the *salons* of the period. See his letter in V. Giraud, *Maîtres de l'Heure* (Paris: Hachette, 1915), I, 55. Loti secretly read quite a lot in fact: see L. Cario, "Pierre Loti aux armées," *Mercure de France,* 1 July 1923, p. 107, and Odette V., *Mon Ami Pierre Loti* (Paris: Flammarion, 1930), pp. 64–5.

33. M. S. van de Verde, *French Fiction of Today,* II (London: Trischler, 1891), 86.

34. V. Giraud, "La Jeunesse de Pierre Loti," *Revue des Deux Mondes,* 1 June 1926, p. 708.

35. Robert de Traz, *Pierre Loti* (Paris, Hachette, 1948), p. 78.

36. See M. Déribéré, "Le Voyage de Pierre Loti à l'Ile de Pâques," *Courier des Messageries Maritimes,* No. 126 (1972), pp. 27–33.

37. See Elfriede Kleinholz, *Impressionismus bei Pierre Loti* (Münster: Langendreer, 1938) for Loti's use of repetition (pp. 26–32), inversion (pp. 33–46), infinitives (pp. 58–61), indefinite vocabulary (pp. 66–67), and metaphor (pp. 67–69).

38. J. Lemaître, *Les Contemporains* (Paris: Lecène-Oudin, 1887), III, 93–94.

39. See letter of Mme Adam of 28 January 1881 in *Journal Intime,* p. 216.

40. P. Bourget, *Etudes et Portraits* (Paris: Plon, 1906), II, 359.

41. This sentimental fetishism is obvious in the structure of much of Loti's work; he begins a story or chapter by describing an object and then evokes people or places associated with it, linking these retrospective impressions with his mood and moral theme; this is seen in the descriptions of the faded flowers Harry Grant brings home from Tahiti, the *livret de marin* in *Mon Frère Yves,* and the various souvenirs of Loti's childhood novels.

Chapter Three

1. Letter of 23 February 1881 in *Journal Intime,* p. 234.

2. Letter of 4 February 1883 in *Journal Intime 1882–85* (Paris, 1930), p. 19. On Loti's friendship with Pouvillon, see R. Lefèvre, *En Marge de Loti,* pp. 113–80.

3. See letter of 10 March 1881 in *Lettres à Mme Adam,* p. 12.

4. *Ibid.,* pp. 20–21.

5. Mme Adam was by no means pleased with Loti and Plumkett's collaboration, considerably cut their script, and regarded *Fleurs d'Ennui* as a failure for Loti: see Keith Millward, "Mme Adam et les Débuts de Pierre Loti," *Cahiers Pierre Loti* June, 1960, pp. 11–16.

6. Undated letter in *Journal Intime,* p. 219. On Loti's acquaintance with Le Cor, see R. Maurice, *En Marge d'Aziyadé,* pp. 32–38, and E. de Crauzat, *Le Vrai Mon Frère Yves* (Paris: Livre Contemporain, 1927), 22 pp. For details of the Le Cors's life and background, see Yves Le Corre, *"Mon Frère Yves à Rosporden,"* *Cahiers Pierre Loti,* March, 1958, pp. 17–21; and for a description of Loti's visits to Rosporden and photographs of the house, see Pierre Kermadec, *Pierre Loti chez mon frère Yves* (Paris: Livre Contemporain, 1927), 56 pp.

7. Letter of 28 July 1880, pp. 175–76.

8. See Loti's letter on Yves being made drunk by his comrades of 8 May 1879, *ibid.,* p. 70.

9. Letter of January, 1883, in *Journal Intime,* p. 17.

10. There is a sketch of Yves in Cl. Farrère, *Cent Dessins de P. Loti,* p. 189, and photographs in R. Maurice, *op.cit.,* pp. 19, 39.

11. In reality, Yves never conquered his addiction to drink; he retired from the navy in 1893 to Rosporden and died in 1927. Loti was annoyed by Yves's continued alcoholism and finally refused even to hear his name mentioned.

12. Entry for 27 October 1883 in the Goncourt *Journal* (Paris: Flammarion, 1956), III, 281.

13. After the failure of *Fleurs d'Ennui* and *Mon Frère Yves* had appeared in the *Revue des Deux Mondes,* Mme Adam was especially pleased to claim *Pêcheur d'Islande* for the *Nouvelle Revue:* see K. Millward, "Mme Adam et les Débuts de Pierre Loti," *Cahiers Pierre Loti,* March, 1961, pp. 20–26.

14. In a note of 21 December 1882 in his *Journal Intime,* he refers to his idea of marrying this Breton girl as "salvation" and "my last true hope" (pp. 3–5) and when she refuses him on 13 December 1884, he speaks of his "vanished dream" (p. 178).

15. Jean Kerleveo has identified the girl as Célestine Floury, sister of

Guillaume Floury, on whom Loti based Yann's character, and found traces of the original people, places and incidents, which occur in Loti's novel: see his articles on "Paimpol et Pierre Loti" in *Cahiers Pierre Loti,* September, 1961, pp. 20–25; March, 1962, pp. 21–26; June, 1962, pp. 21–25; October, 1962, pp. 21–28; and his volume *Paimpol et son Terroir* (Rennes: Simon, 1971), 97 pp. As further proof of Loti's realism, Louis Barthou quotes in *Pêcheur d'Islande: Etude et Analyse* (Paris: Mellottée, 1929), pp. 357–59, Captain Huchet de Guermeur's reply to Loti's inquiries about Breton marriages and the sunsets and fishing procedures in Iceland waters. An account of the novel's composition (pp. 29–53) and an analysis of its story (pp. 55–209), and characters (pp. 211–57) can also be found in this work.

16. Letter of March, 1885, in *Lettres à Mme Adam,* p. 53.

17. A sketch of Yann can be seen in Cl. Farrère, *Cent Dessins de P. Loti,* p. 199.

18. R. Doumic, *Ecrivains d'Aujourd'hui* (Paris: Perrin, 1894), p. 119.

19. H. Bordeaux, *Ames Modernes* (Paris: Perrin, 1895), p. 108.

Chapter Four

1. See E. D'Auvergne, pp. 99–101.

2. See Loti's letter of 9 December 1883 in *Lettres à Mme Adam,* pp. 32–33, and his letter to Daudet in the *Revue Maritime,* February, 1950, pp. 176–77.

3. See *Lettres à Mme Adam,* p. 34, and *Journal Intime 1882–85,* p. 130.

4. *Correspondance inédite,* p. 192.

5. Letter of 7 August 1885, *ibid.,* p. 195.

6. *Ibid.*

7. Letter of 8 October 1885, *ibid.,* p. 205.

8. Letter of 6 November 1885, *ibid.,* p. 214.

9. Letter of 13 November 1885, *ibid.,* p. 216.

10. The Japanese were in fact somewhat annoyed at this contrived view of Japan's decadence: see A. Moulis, "Loti au Japon," *Cahiers Pierre Loti,* September, 1958, p. 9. Nevertheless, a monument was inaugurated in Nagasaki in 1950 to mark the centenary of Loti's birth.

Chapter Five

1. See *Lettres à Mme Adam,* p. 43.

2. *Ibid.,* p. 94.

3. Sacha Guitry was to comment on a visit to Loti's house: "The man

was married, the naval officer less so—and Loti never," in *La Maison de Loti* (Paris: Amis d'Edouard, 1931), p. 8.

4. Mme Loti lived with her husband during his four years' service on the Bidassoa and attended his presentation at the Académie, but as his travels took him more and more away from home for long periods she increasingly returned to Bordeaux to stay with her mother; she visited him with their son later on at Istanbul and Toulon and even later came to Rochefort for their grandson's baptism, but essentially their lives were spent apart. She was an intelligent, kindly woman, with a slight hearing impediment due to her miscarriage, who supported Loti's way of life with great understanding and effaced herself completely after his death. She died in April, 1940, aged 86.

5. Entry for 21 February 1888 in *Journal,* Vol. 3, 757. On Loti's homosexual tendencies, see K. Millward, *L'Oeuvre de Pierre Loti et l'Esprit Fin de Siècle* (Paris: Nizet, 1955), pp. 156–68. Laurent de Tailhade satirized these tendencies in Loti, referring to him as *ma tante Loti,* in his *Poèmes Aristophanesques* (Paris: Mercure de France, 1904), pp. 48, 51, 129. Loti's life among the simple and handsome local people and sailors at Hendaye caused scandalous gossip among some of his neighbors there too (see V. Détharé, "Pierre Loti à Hendaye," *Nouvelles Littéraires,* 27 July 1929). For a description of him at this time, see Robert de Montesquiou, *Les Pas Effacés* (Paris: Emile-Paul, 1923), III, 44.

6. A sketch of this banquet by Bellenger can be found in *L'Illustration,* 21 April 1888, p. 280. The old French menus for the banquet can be seen in P. Lasturel, "Pierre Loti intime," *Revue Hebdomadaire,* 5 April 1902, pp. 65–67.

7. On Carmen Silva see R. Scheffer, "La Reine Carmen Sylva," *Mercure de France,* 16 April 1916, pp. 577–602, and R. Lefèvre, "Carmen Silva et Pierre Loti," *Deutschland-Frankreich,* no. 6 (1943) pp. 66–81. The first contains some interesting details of her life including her visits to Queen Victoria at Balmoral and her participation in the Welsh Eisteddfod; the second contains some of the correspondence between her and Loti.

8. Letter of 15 April 1891 in *Lettres à Mme Adam,* p. 117.

9. See K. Millward, *op. cit.,* pp. 161–63. Loti was to write in his diary of 1893: "Léo is the one whose soul is most like my own and the closest to me, a real brotherly friend who understands me completely and whom I would like to have near me when I die," (*Cahiers Pierre Loti,* June, 1965, p. 6). Jean Lorrain was to attest to Léo's virile handsomeness on a visit to Loti in August 1896: see his *Lettres à Ma Mère* (Paris: Excelsior, 1926), p. 132.

10. A moth fluttering around Loti one evening soon after her death was later seen by him as the soul of this aunt who had helped him in his child-

hood with his butterfly and moth collection: see "Journal Intime Inédit," *Cahiers Pierre Loti*, September, 1958, pp. 3–4. Loti occasionally had such thoughts of reincarnation (see below note 8 of Chapter 7) but he never really defined them.

11. Loti almost did not go to Venice because of his irritation at the comments on his timidity at his first visit to Sinaia, which Helen Vacaresco had given to an Hungarian journalist and that had appeared in the European press. It was partly through trying to teach Mlle Vacaresco a lesson by sending her an offensive model of herself and partly by defending Carmen Silva that Loti incurred King Charles's anger and his banishment from the Rumanian court. Relations between Loti and the Queen were thus interrupted until 1908, when they were resumed up to her death in 1915 with exchanges of letters, books, and photographs. For details of these and Loti's translations of some of the Queen's tales, see Leopold Stern, *Pierre Loti et Carmen Sylva* (Paris: Grasset, 1931), 183 pp.

12. Loti's diary account of this third meeting with the Queen and a photograph of them can be found in the *Cahiers Pierre Loti*, March, 1960, pp. 3–8.

Chapter Six

1. On Loti's election to the Académie, see Goncourt's entries in his *Journal* for 31 October and 12 December 1889 and also Henri Borgeaud, "L'élection de Pierre Loti à l'Académie Française," *Cahiers Pierre Loti*, December, 1956, pp. 7–9. The Countess Diane de Beausacq helped Loti at both his attempts to enter the Académie by her contacts with Sully Prudhomme and Camille Doucet. Even so, Loti only received the eighteen votes he needed at the sixth ballot for Feuillet's seat; he had already failed in his candidature for Augier's seat, which Daudet and Goncourt had encouraged him to present the previous year, by withdrawing in favor of Freycinet. Zola was irritated at being beaten by Loti, and Barrès was to condemn his election in a malicious article in the *Figaro* on 9 April 1892. On Loti's reception at the Académie, see K. Millward, *op. cit.,* pp. 78–79, and on Zola's and Goncourt's reactions, see the latter's *Journal,* 7 and 11 April 1892. See below note 9 of Chapter 9.

2. Quoted in Elizabeth Stevenson, *Lafcadio Hearn* (New York, 1961), p. 149. For Loti's influence on Hearn, see Albert Mordell, *Discoveries— Essays on Lafcadio Hearn* (Tokyo, 1964), pp. 104–8.

3. Preface to P. Loti, *Impressions* (London: Constable, 1898), p. 19. For James's other review of Loti, see his *Essays in London and Elsewhere* (London: Constable, 1893).

4. See F. Charles-Roux, "La Mission Patenôtre au Maroc," *Cahiers Pierre Loti,* September, 1958, pp. 19–23.

5. See N. Serban, *op. cit.*, pp. 122–23.

6. See in this context Loti's interview for *Le Journal* quoted in N. Serban, *op. cit.*, p. 124.

7. Loti was to write to Mme Adam in 1895 that the last pages of *Jérusalem* were totally sincere but very bad even so (*Lettres à Mme Adam*, p. 139). On Loti's reactions to the sites of the Holy Land, see Marie-Jeanne Hublard, *L'attitude religieuse de Pierre Loti* (Fribourg: St. Paul, 1945), 168 pp; she defines Loti's reactions as emotional and autosuggestive (p. 96), and compares them to Renan's more rational approach (pp. 163–64).

8. On the composition of *Ramuntcho,* see André Moulis, "Genèse de Ramuntcho," *Annales de la Faculté des Lettres et Sciences Humaines de Toulouse,* Littératures XII (November, 1965), 49–78.

9. "Journal Intime Inédit, avril-juin 1893," *Cahiers Pierre Loti,* June, 1964, p. 7.

10. *Ibid.,* December, 1965, p. 5.

11. *Ibid.,* June, 1966, pp. 5–6.

12. It is claimed that Loti was the father of three illegitimate Basque children; one died in infancy; the other two, Edmond and Raymond or Ramuntcho, were his sons by a Basque mistress named Crucita Gainza he frequented in autumn, 1894, and lodged outside Rochefort thereafter. The *faubourg* family scene described in "Fragments d'un Journal Intime" (*Quelques Aspects du Vertige Mondial*) might well refer to this aspect of Loti's life. Ramuntcho thus seems to have had a physical reality.

13. E. Friderich, *Baskenland und Basken bei Pierre Loti* (Würzburg: Mayr, 1934), p. 10.

14. The play was performed on 2 November 1898, but partly composed during the writing of *Ramuntcho.* The fact that Loti distorts the Renaudins' history to make Judith, who was only eleven years old and renounced her faith in 1685, the savior of her family on Oleron when the Edict of Nantes is revoked, reflects his own admiration of the Huguenots' piety. On Loti's treatment of his ancestors' history, see J. W. Marmelstein, "Les Ancêtres de Pierre Loti en Hollande," *Neophilologus,* 1928, pp. 180–87.

15. Details of Loti's life at Hendaye can be found in René Cuzacq, *Les Ecrivains du Pays Basque et Bayonnais* (Mont de Marsan: Lacoste, 1951), pp. 35–53, and also Frédéric A. Chassériau, *Mes Souvenirs Sur Pierre Loti et Francis Jammes* (Paris: Plon, 1937), pp. 40–50.

16. This title was proposed by Loti's friend, Emile Vedel; Loti had originally called the section on Travancore *Dans l'Inde encore Indienne,* but Brunetière altered it for the *Revue.*

17. Loti was to confide to Mme Adam on 15 April 1900 that he had "gained some insight into the peace and eternity at the heart of the esoteric Brahminism I admire" (*Lettres à Mme Adam*, p. 152).

Chapter Seven

1. Loti's diary account of his experiences was published in the February, 1955, to December, 1956, issues of the *Cahiers Pierre Loti.*

2. Similar gruesome incidents are found later in Loti's Chinese play *La Fille du Ciel,* where bodies and heads strew the blood-spattered scene in the last act. It could be said that there is a certain sadistic fascination for such horrors in the artistic detachment with which he conveys such local atmosphere, and moves, often shocks, his reader—as in his account of the Annam war and later in *Suprêmes Visions d'Orient.*

3. Loti apparently had some difficulty in writing the novel at Istanbul and was not very satisfied with it after he had finished it: see Cl. Farrère, *Pierre Loti quand je l'ai connu,* p. 32. When it was completed, the *Revue*'s editor, Brunetière, feared Loti's title would offend the Japanese and altered it to *Escales au Japon,* 1902, despite Loti's protests: see "Lettres de F. Brunetière à P. Loti," *Le Correspondant,* 25 May 1926, pp. 516–17.

4. See Guy de Pourtalès, "Trois Jours chez Loti," *Cahiers Pierre Loti,* June, 1964, pp. 8–10 and Alice Louis-Barthou, "La Maison Enchantée," *Mercure de Flandre,* January-February, 1931, pp. 15–20. Loti would place flowers from her real tomb on his replica of it after each of his visits to Turkey. Photographs of the mosque and Loti in it can be found in R. L. Graeme Ritchie, *Pierre Loti* (London: Nelson, 1930), p. 137; in *Images de Pierre Loti,* prés F. Duhourcau, G. Mauberger, H. Talvart & Cl. Farrère (La Rochelle: Editions d'Art Ramuntcho, 1935), 117 pp.; G. Mauberger, "La Maison de Pierre Loti," *L'Illustration,* 8 September 1906, pp. 159–61; and H. Borgeaud, "La Maison de Pierre Loti," *Revue Maritime,* January, 1952, pp. 34–49. Loti, like T. E. Lawrence, showed his Arab sympathies by dressing in Arab clothes and enjoyed immensely posing for visitors in Arab or Bedouin disguise in his mosque; he also prostrated himself in prayer and meditation there; his only regret was that its *mihrab* did not face exactly east toward Mecca.

5. Queen Nathalie had previously asked Loti to Bidart and Biarritz and her signed photograph was to be found with those of other queens on his desk at Rochefort. For an account of the tricks Loti and Mme Adam played on each other when she stayed in the smugglers' tower at Hendaye or Loti visited her at Gif on the Golfe Juan, see Antoine Albalat, *Souvenirs de la Vie Littéraire* (Paris: Fayard, 1921), pp. 284–85, and Gilbert Charles, "Pierre Loti Intime," *Le Figaro,* 12 June 1923, Loti's Chinese party, at which both dress and food were as authentic as possible and Mme Adam played the Empress, is described in Judith Gautier, *Les Parfums de la Pagode* (Paris: Fasquelle, 1919), pp. 141–49.

6. A description of Loti's arrival on the "Vautour" with abundant

details of his small stature and saturnine expression can be found in Cl. Farrère, *Pierre Loti quand je l'ai connu,* pp. 10–14.

7. Impressions of Loti in Istanbul are provided by his visitors there, Gabriel de la Rochefoucauld, in *Constantinople avec Loti* (Paris: Editions de France, 1928), pp. 66–88, and Henri de Régnier, in "A Stamboul au Temps de Loti," *Revue des Deux Mondes,* 15 June 1926, pp. 826–46. Loti's wife and son, Mme Adam, and Sarah Bernhardt also visited him during his stay. The grandiose baptism, costing ten thousand francs, of Loti's angora cat Belkis took place on board the "Vautour" at this time; like Loti's *fêtes* at Rochefort, such expensive frivolity caused quite a scandal back in France: see Cl. Farrère, "La Chatte Baptisée," *Le Gaulois,* 16 June 1923.

8. Comparisons of Loti's record of their meetings in his diary and their correspondence and the novel's text are to be found with many other details concerning the novel's composition in Raymonde Lefêvre, *Les Désenchantées de Pierre Loti* (Paris: Malfère, 1939), 141 pp. See also Pierre Briquet, *op. cit.,* pp. 378–436.

9. Loti referred again to the plight of sophisticated harem women in a paper entitled *La Femme Turque* read at the Salle de la Vie Féminine in spring, 1914, and published in *Quelques Aspects du Vertige Mondial.*

10. The precise source of Loti's information on Turkish harems was suspected by some critics when the novel appeared; for Nouryé Neyr-el-Nissa fled, disguised as the elderly mother of her sister and friend Marcelle to Belgrade, Venice, and finally Paris in January, 1906, and wrote about their escape and the difficulties they encountered en route in her articles on "Notre Evasion du Harem" in *Le Figaro,* 19 and 27 February and 5 March 1906; these were mentioned by E. Ledrain in his review of the novel in *L'Illustration,* 28 July 1906, p. 66, where he asked whether the heroines of the articles and the novel were not the same. Nouryé's sister, Hadidjé Zennour, was to attempt to prove the accuracy of Loti's realism in the novel by revealing her identity as Zeyneb in it and confirming that, even though her sister (who was Mélek) was still alive, their cousin Leyla (or Djénane) lay buried at Eyub, in her article "La vérité vraie sur les *Désenchantées,*" *Le Figaro,* 21 December 1909. Later, after Loti's death, Leyla came alive at last as Marc Hélys and published their correspondence with Loti, photographs of the three of them, and details of their complex schemes to retain Loti's confidence in *L'Envers d'un Roman: Le Secret des Désenchantées révélé par celle qui fut Djénane* (Paris: Perrin, 1924), 283 pp.; Claude Farrère was to protest at her unashamed vanity in revealing the trick played on Loti and her bad influence on the novel in "Une Mystification Littéraire," *Le Gaulois,* 18 September 1923. Publishing a photograph of Loti with the two veiled Noury sisters, Mme Hélys later denied

they had deceived him and asserted they had simply followed up his desire to get to know them ("Pierre Loti mon beau souvenir," *Le Figaro,* 10 June 1933). Mme Hélys was clearly reluctant, however, to enlighten Loti on their intrigue even though she was aware of his emotional reaction to it; she had in fact been present at the Salle de la Vie Féminine when Djénane's last letter to Lhéry was read out (see *supra,* note 6) and witnessed the grief this caused him. Affinities between Aziyadé and the *désenchantées* had even prompted him to search for the latter on his visit to Turkey in 1910: see *Suprêmes Visions d'Orient* and also A. Cillières, "Souvenirs sur Pierre Loti," *Revue de France,* 15 January 1934, pp. 253–61.

11. Loti's fear of ageing and concern with death found expression after his visit to Egypt in the postcards he sent out to friends showing on one half a photograph of the mummified profile of Ramses II and on the other a profile of himself in a similar pose with the words "not yet mummified" written on it (see G. de la Rochefoucauld, *op. cit.,* p. 3). Loti always admired Ramses II because he had been renowned for his athletic build; he wore among the many rings he used to wear one said to have belonged to the pharaoh because he thought at one time, on account of the similarity of their profiles, that he was a reincarnation of him (see L. F. de Robert, *De Loti à Proust* (Paris: Flammarion, 1928), p. 238.

Chapter Eight

1. See *Le Château de la Belle au Bois Dormant* and *Quelques Aspects du Vertige Mondial* for details of his visit. He was the guest of both the French Ambassador, M. Cambon, who gave a dinner on 9 July 1909 in his honor and of the Orientalist Lord Redesdale, at whose home at Batsford Park he stayed for a few days.

2. See A. Thomazi, "Julien Viaud, officier de marine," *Revue Maritime* February, 1950, pp. 165–81.

3. See Comtesse L. Ostrorog, *Pierre Loti à Constantinople* (Paris: E. Figuière, 1927), 189 pp., for a general account of Loti's stay in Istanbul.

4. Loti lived here, at Divan-Youlou no. 1, under the name of Daoud and later assumed the name Durand when he entered the French Hospital: see A. Cillière, "Souvenirs sur Pierre Loti," *Revue de France,* 1 January 1934, pp. 67–90.

5. Alphonse Cillière, in whose residence Loti stayed, claims that there was nothing seriously wrong with him and that it was his low morale rather than his influenza which required a cure (*op. cit., Revue de France,* 1 January 1934, p. 86 and 15 January 1934, p. 241).

6. See below note 6 of Chapter 9.

7. His stay in America is described in *Quelques Aspects du Vertige*

Mondial. The play, written in collaboration with the Wagnerian and Orientalist Judith Gautier and for Sarah Bernhardt, who was originally to play the leading role in it, was never performed in France but did appear in the March to May, 1911, issues of the *Revue des Deux Mondes* and was published by Calmann-Lévy that year. On Loti's collaboration with Judith Gautier, see Mathilde Camacho, *Judith Gautier: sa vie et son oeuvre* (Paris: Droz, 1939), pp. 158–66. The play's action concerns the vain attempts of the Tartar Emperor of Peking to stop the conflict between his alien dynasty and the Ming Empress at Nanking; he halts the war between them and spares the lives of his Ming prisoners, including the Empress, whom he wants to marry as a final reconciliation, but she prefers suicide to betraying the loyalty of her army and people. Full of spectacular tableaux and melodramatic gestures and incidents, the play's merits rest on the increasingly tense confrontation between Emperor and Empress right up to that in the final scene.

8. In 1899 Loti had gone to Berlin to see the Kaiser and seek a *rapprochement* between France and Germany against Britain; the visit almost cost him his friendship with Mme Adam and was a failure. Loti did not see the Kaiser and disliked Berlin intensely: see his article, "Je revenais de chez l'ennemi," *Le Figaro,* 19 April 1900. As German militarism increased in the first decade of the century, Loti soon changed his earlier view.

9. See Louis Cario, "Pierre Loti aux Armées," *Mercure de France,* 1, July 1923, pp. 97–110, and Franchet d'Esperey's article in *Mercure de Flandre,* January–February, 1931, pp. 98–103.

10. See Odette V., *Mon Ami Pierre Loti, passim,* for a young woman's impressions of Loti's morose outlook and self-consciousness about his aging at this time.

11. See Cl. Farrère, *Ma Dernière Visite à Loti* (Abbeville: Amis d'Edouard, 1923), particularly pp. 35–36 and 72–73. In an article on "Loti et Aziyadé," G. Mauberger was to describe how Loti was cheered up after illness in June, 1922, by receiving letters from Turkey containing flowers from Aziyadé's tomb (*Le Figaro,* 5 June 1926).

12. See *Lettres à Mme Adam,* pp. 244, 247–48, and K. Millward, "Mme Adam et les Débuts de Loti," *Cahiers Pierre Loti,* June, 1961, p. 27.

13. Details of Loti's last days can be found in Gaston Mauberger's article, "Les Derniers Jours de Loti," in *Images de Pierre Loti,* prés. F. Duhourcau, G. Mauberger, & H. Talvart, pp. 52–80.

14. See Yvan Delteil, *L'Ile d'Oleron,* pp. 96–97.

15. See for details of Loti's will: M. E. de Bonneuil, "La Maison des Aieules," *Revue des Deux Mondes,* 1 September 1934, pp. 223–28.

16. His request was not carried out and the house at Rochefort has been a museum since his son's death in 1969.

17. An account of the funeral is given in "Les Obsèques de Pierre Loti," *Le Figaro,* 17 June 1923.

Chapter 9

1. By 1905 *Pêcheur d'Islande* was in its 261st edition, *Mon Frère Yves* in its 93rd. *Le Mariage de Loti* in its 74th, *Ramuntcho* in its 65th, and *Le Roman d'un Spahi* in its 56th (V. Giraud, *op. cit.,* p. 16). For details of translations *see Bibliography,* 2. A dramatization of *Pêcheur d'Islande* by Loti and Louis Tiercelin with music by Guy Ropartz ran for twenty performances at the Grand Théâtre in Paris beginning 19 February 1893; *Madame Chrysanthème* was made into a lyrical comedy of four acts by G. Hartmann and A. Alexandre with music by A. Messager, and performed at the Théâtre Lyrique on 30 January 1893; a lyrical poem in four acts, *Le Spahi,* by L. Gallet and A. Alexandre, with music by L. Lambert, began at the Opéra Comique on 18 October 1897; *Le Mariage de Loti* was presented as *L'Ile du Rêve,* a Polynesian idyll in three acts, at the Opéra Comique on 23 March 1898 with music by R. Hahn and lyrics by Loti himself, André Alexandre, and Georges Hartmann; and Loti's play in five acts from *Ramuntcho* was performed at the Odéon on 29 February 1908 with music by Gabriel Pierné.

2. See P. Jourda, *L'Exotisme dans la Littérature Française depuis Chateaubriand* (Montpellier: Presses Universitaires de France, 1956), 294 pp., and also Hassan el Nouty, *Le Proche-Orient dans la Littérature Française de Nerval à Barrès* (Paris: Nizet, 1958), 338 pp.

3. See Mario Praz, *The Romantic Agony* (London: Oxford University Press, 1933), 454 pp.

4. See A. E. Carter, *The Idea of Decadence in French Literature, 1830–1900* (Toronto University Press, 1958), 154 pp., and G. Michaud, *le Message Poétique du Symbolisme* (Paris: Nizet, 1947), 3 vols.

5. On this, see the interesting article of Lucien Duplessy, "Pierre Loti a-t-il fait des romans?" in the *Grande Revue,* December, 1925, pp. 219–41.

6. Loti's attachment to Aziyadé, her tombstone and Turkey in general, and the decoration of his house with relics from his visits overseas can be considered as part of this pseudo-religious, sentimental, and temporal fetishism derived from his insecurity and exotic cult of himself. Robert de Montesquiou was in fact to refer to the exotic furnishings of Loti's house as *un bouquet fardé*—a bouquet of flowers kept to look fresh by being touched up with paint *(Le Gaulois du Dimanche,* 24–25 November, 1906). See note 41 of Chapter 2.

7. See R. M. Griffiths, *The Reactionary Revolution* (London: Constable, 1966), 393 pp; M. Tison-Braun, *La Crise de l'Humanisme 1890–1914*

(Paris: Nizet, 1958), 520 pp; and A. Billy, *L'Epoque 1900* (Paris: Tallandier, 1951), 484 pp.

8. See *supra* note 32 of *Chapter Two.*

9. G. Lanson, *Histoire de la Littérature Française* (Paris: Hachette, 1912), p. 1088.

10. In his tribute to Feuillet, Loti declared that, while the crudity and cynicism of Naturalism was a Parisian *fin de siècle* phenomenon of the century's oversophistication, Feuillet's idealism would live on; for Man's ideals were eternal and were beginning to come into focus once more beyond the crude, vulgar aspects of life the Realists and Naturalists had concentrated on (*Discours de Réception* (Paris: C. Lévy, 1892), pp. 50–51). Such a declaration angered both Zola and Loti's friends Daudet and Goncourt, and Loti was to write to Zola apologizing for any offense he had given in his speech (see L. F. de Robert, *op. cit.,* pp. 62–63). Loti was later, however, to condemn the cruder, Naturalistic elements in his own early works—much of which had been cut by Mme Adam or Calmann-Lévy—as part of his revolt against the amorality and skepticism of the century's unhealthy oversophistication (see Cl. Farrère, *Pierre Loti quand je l'ai connu,* p. 46, and Odette V., *op. cit.,* pp. 29–30).

11. Roland Barthes in fact calls Loti a "dandyish hippy" in his revolt against Western civilization: see "Le nom d'Aziyadé", *Critique* (February, 1972), p. 115.

Selected Bibliography

PRIMARY SOURCES

All Loti's works were published by Calmann-Lévy, Paris, and his major works have been frequently republished by them since. An eleven-volume edition of his collected works up to 1905 including his dramatizations was published by Calmann-Lévy in the years 1893 to 1911. *Aziyadé, Mon Frère Yves, Pêcheur d'Islande, Ramuntcho*, and *Les Désenchantées* are available in the *Livre de Poche* collection. English school editions of some of these texts exist in the old Rivingtons and Heath series and, more recently, editions of *Pêcheur d'Islande* and *Ramuntcho* by N. Scarlyn Wilson were published by G. Harrap, London, in 1960 and 1961, respectively.

1. Novels and Short Stories
Aziyadé, 1879
Le Mariage de Loti, 1880
Le Roman d'un Spahi, 1881
Fleurs d'Ennui, 1883
Mon Frère Yves, 1883
Pêcheur d'Islande, 1886
Madame Chrysanthème, 1888
Le Roman d'un Enfant, 1890
Livre de la Pitié et de la Mort, 1891
Fantôme d'Orient, 1892
Matelot, 1893
Ramuntcho, 1897
La Troisième Jeunesse de Madame Prune, 1905
Les Désenchantées, 1906
Prime Jeunesse, 1919

2. Travel Essays
Propos d'Exil, 1887
Japoneries d'Automne, 1889
Au Maroc, 1890
L'Exilée 1893

Le Désert, 1895
Jérusalem, 1895
La Galilée, 1896
Figures et Choses qui passaient, 1898
Reflets sur la Sombre Route, 1899
Les Derniers Jours de Pékin, 1902
L'Inde sans les Anglais, 1903
Vers Ispahan, 1904
La Mort de Philae, 1908
Le Château de la Belle au Bois Dormant, 1910
Un Pèlerin d'Angkor, 1912

3. Political Writings
Turquie Agonisante, 1913
La Grande Barbarie, 1915
La Hyène Enragée, 1916
Quelques Aspects du Vertige Mondial, 1917
L'Horreur Allemande, 1918
La Mort de notre chère France en Orient, 1920
Suprêmes Visions d'Orient, 1921

4. Plays
Pêcheur d'Islande, 1893
Judith Renaudin, 1898
Ramuntcho, 1908
La Fille du Ciel, 1911

5. Correspondence
Lettres à Mme J. Adam, 1880–1922 (Paris: Plon, 1924). 248 pp. *Correspon-dance inédite, 1865–1904*, ed. N. Duvignau & N. Serban (Paris: C.-Lévy, 1929), 246 pp.

6. Diary
Sections of Loti's diary relating to the years 1867–1881 and 1882–1885 were published by Calmann-Lévy in 1925 and 1929, respectively. Fragments from it describing Loti's earlier years can be found in *Un Jeune Officier Pauvre*, 1923, and extracts from it concerning later years have since appeared in the *Cahiers Pierre Loti*, Toulouse, as well as in the work quoted below of O. Valence and K. Millward.

7. Translations
Virtually all Loti's works were translated; T. Werner Laurie of London published the following translations of his major works:

Jerusalem, tr. W. P. Baines, 1915.
A Tale of the Pyrenees, tr. W. P. Baines, 1923.
India, tr. R. Sherard, 1906.
Madame Prune, tr. S. R. C. Plimsoll, 1919.
Egypt, tr. W. P. Baines, 1909.
Siam, tr. W. P. Baines, 1913.
War, tr. M. Laurie, 1917.
A fuller list of translations into English, German, and Italian can be found,
in F. Mallet, *Pierre Loti, son oeuvre* (Paris: Ed. Nouvelle Revue Critique,
1923), pp. 57–58.

8. Loti's Correspondence
Lettres à Mme Juliette Adam, 1880–1922 (Paris: Plon, 1924), 248 pp.
Correspondance inédite, 1865–1904, ed. N. Duvignau & N. Serban (Paris:
Calmann-Lévy, 1929), 246 pp.

SECONDARY SOURCES

BRIQUET, P. *Pierre Loti et l'Orient* (Paris: Zeluck, 1946), 614 pp. A de-
  tailed analysis of Loti's association with and interest in the Islamic
  world.
BRODIN, P. *Loti* (Montreal: Parizeau, 1945), 384 pp. A shortish,
  simplified account of Loti's career and writings.
D'AUVERGNE, E. B. *Pierre Loti, the Romance of a Great Writer* (London:
  Werner Laurie, 1926), 253 pp. An informative even if oversentimental
  biography.
EKSTRÖM, G. *Evasions et Désespérances de Pierre Loti* (Gothenburg:
  Gumperts, 1953), 136 pp. A detailed thesis on aspects of Loti's spiritual
  struggles.
FARRÈRE, CL. *Cent Dessins de Pierre Loti* (Paris: Arrault, 1948), 217
  pp. An interesting review of Loti the artist in relation to his writings on
  his travels overseas.
FLOTTES, P. *Le Drame Intérieur de Pierre Loti* (Paris: Courrier Littéraire,
  1937), 270 pp. A somewhat superficial but occasionally enlightening
  study of Loti's inner conflicts as reflected in his work.
HUBLARD, J. M. *L'Attitude Religieuse de Pierre Loti* (Fribourg: St Paul,
  1945), 168 pp. A penetrating thesis on Loti's quest for faith.
KLEINHOLZ, E. *Impressionismus bei Pierre Loti* (Münster: Langendreer,
  1938), 75 pp. An analysis in some depth of Loti's particular impressionism in his style.
LEFÈVRE, R. *La Vie Inquiète de Pierre Loti* (Paris: Soc. Franç.

d'Editions Littéraires et Techniques, 1934), 252 pp. A well-informed study of Loti's anguished life as seen through his work.

MILLWARD, K. *L'Oeuvre de Pierre Loti et l'Esprit Fin de Siècle* (Paris: Nizet, 1955), 371 pp. An account of Loti's life and work in relation to their *fin de siècle* context.

SERBAN, N. *Pierre Loti, sa vie, son oeuvre* (Paris: Presses Françaises, 1924), 372 pp. An informative, early attempt at a comprehensive study of Loti's career.

TRAZ, R. DE *Pierre Loti* (Paris: Hachette, 1948), 187 pp. A short, general review of the main themes of Loti's work.

VALENCE, O. & VIAUD, S. *La Famille de Pierre Loti ou l'Education Passionnée* (Paris: C.-Lévy, 1940), 231 pp. An intimate account of Loti's early life and relations with his family.

FURTHER SOURCES OF INFORMATION

The special issues of the *Mercure de Flandre,* Paris, January–February, 1931, 208 pp., on "Pierre Loti vu par ses Contemporains" and of the *Revue Maritime* (Paris: Ministre de la Marine), February, 1950, pp.145–316, on "Pierre Loti" are useful sources of additional information on Loti's life. The *Bulletins Trimestriels de l'Association Internationale des Amis de Pierre Loti* from 1933 to 1951 and the *Cahiers Pierre Loti* since 1952 should be consulted too by the more serious scholar. Details of more specialized studies concerning particular aspects of Loti's life or specific works can be found in this volume in the individual chapter notes; a longer bibliography with details of other sources of information, studies, and articles on Loti's life and work can be found in N. Serban, *op. cit.,* pp. 338–63, and K. Millward, *op. cit.,* pp. 342–66, as well as in Hugo Thieme's *Bibliographie de la Littérature Française* (Paris: Droz, 1933), pp. 181–85.

Index